PRODUCING
VIDEO PODCASTS

PRODUCING VIDEO PODCASTS

A Guide for Media Professionals

RICHARD HARRINGTON
and MARK WEISER
with RHED PIXEL

AMSTERDAM • BOSTON • HEIDELBERG • LONDON • NEW YORK • OXFORD
PARIS • SAN DIEGO • SAN FRANCISCO • SINGAPORE • SYDNEY • TOKYO
Focal Press is an imprint of Elsevier

Cover Design:	Ian Pullens
RSS feed icon:	Peter Marquardt <podcast@lemotox.de>
Photography:	Emmanuel Etim, Liang Cai, Ian Pullens, Richard Harrington, and Mark Weiser
Technical Reviewers:	Phillip Hodgetts, Jason Van Orden, Kristopher Smith, Lee Gibbons, Nicole Haddock, and Megan Tytler
Contributors:	Jason Van Orden, Paul Vogelzang, Nicole Haddock, and Emmanuel Etim
Senior Acquisitions Editor:	Paul Temme
Publishing Services Manager:	George Morrison
Project Manager:	Andre Cuello
Assistant Editor:	Chris Simpson
Marketing Manager:	Rebecca Pease

Focal Press is an imprint of Elsevier
30 Corporate Drive, Suite 400, Burlington, MA 01803, USA
Linacre House, Jordan Hill, Oxford OX2 8DP, UK

∞ Recognizing the importance of preserving what has been written, Elsevier prints its books on acid-free paper whenever possible.

Library of Congress Cataloging-in-Publication Data
Application submitted

British Library Cataloguing-in-Publication Data
A catalogue record for this book is available from the British Library.

ISBN: 978-0-240-81029-4

For information on all Focal Press publications
visit our website at www.books.elsevier.com

08 09 10 11   6 5 4 3 2 1

Printed in Canada

Dedications

To my wife
Meghan, whose love and patience makes all things possible.

To my children
Michael and Colleen, who give my life meaning.

To my parents
For teaching me to work hard and treat others fairly.
—Richard Harrington

To Casey for all her love and support.
To Brooke and Brian for bringing a smile to my face every day.
—Mark Weiser

CONTENTS

Acknowledgements

The authors would like to thank the following individuals and organizations for their generous contributions to this book and our podcasting knowledge.

Gary Adcock	Ron Hansen	Chris Phrommayon
Jim Ball	Serena Herr	Iva Radivojevic
Steve Bayes	Phillip Hodgetts	Scott Rekdal
Joel Bell	Scott Kelby	The Staff of RHED Pixel
Richard Burns	Steve Kilisky	Scott Sheppard
Robbie Carman	Ben Kozuch	Kathy Siler
Dorothy Cox	David Lawrence	Chris Simpson
Creative COW	Logan Leabo	Doug Smith
Bob Donlon	Dennis McGonnagle	Kristopher Smith
Mannie Frances	Stephen Menick	Sound Mind & Body Gym
Michelle Gallina	Dominic Milano	Douglas Spotted Eagle
Eric Garulay	Patricia Montesion	Kourtnaye Sturgeon
Barbara Gavin	David Moser	Paul Temme
Alexandra Gebhart	John Nack	Jason Van Orden
Lee Gibbons	Mark Petracca	Paul Vogelzang
Matt Gottshalk	Dave Potasznik	Terry White
Jeff Greenberg	Gary-Paul Prince	Tim Wilson

INTRODUCTION

Who this Book is For

This book is written for those who need to create professional-level podcasts. We set out to write a book that would offer expert-level advice on all aspects of video podcasting. We realize most of you reading this will have diverse backgrounds, so we will attempt to deliver information at two levels.

The body of the book will present you with the most essential information, richly illustrated, with straightforward advice. Interspersed throughout the book you'll find several tips and sidebars. This information serves two purposes. First, it offers advanced information to let you go deeper on a topic, and second, it points out additional resources if you lack experience with a topic.

Whether you are a video pro, a multimedia developer, or a communications professional, this guide is written to help you. We wanted to create a book that addressed the diverse requirements of podcasting. We also wanted to straighten out several misperceptions and bad practices that we have encountered. If you like your books to be based on real-world experience, this is the book for you.

What You'll Learn

We have structured this book to follow the path of professionally produced podcasts. We *highly* recommend that you read this book's chapters in order. We will build upon the information from one chapter to the next. Here's the journey we'll take together.

The Evolution of Podcasting

Chapter 1—The Business Case for Podcasting. Learn how to explain podcasting accurately to your clients as well as how podcasting is evolving. We'll explore scenarios where podcasting is effective as well as reasons not to podcast.

Chapter 2—What Podcasting Is and Is Not. We will offer a clear understanding of what a podcast is and how it works, as well as the technology options available for podcast playback.

The Production of Podcasts

Chapter 3—Preproduction. This chapter covers important decisions about determining your production needs as well as budgeting your show. Learn practical advice for mapping your production and working with talent.

Chapter 4—Production: Lighting and Sound. Learn how to achieve professional lighting with an emphasis on value and portability. We'll also address strategies to record the best sound for your podcast.

Chapter 5—Production: Videography. Learn the key features you'll need in a video camera. We pay close attention to the evolution of tapeless acquisition and HD video. We also offer a specific packing list to help you bring the most important gear to your podcast shoot.

The Postproduction of Podcasts

Chapter 6—Acquiring Additional Sources. This chapter points out useful ways to add visuals to your story. Learn how to work with photos and stock footage as well as practical tips for motion graphics. You'll also discover several options for using music legally in your podcast.

Chapter 7—Editing Considerations. Putting all of your pieces together takes skill and experiences. We share several lessons learned from having produced thousands of video podcasts.

Chapter 8—Encoding the Podcast. Learn how to create compatible digital files that will work on a podcast. Achieve smaller file sizes and better image clarity with our practical advice on video compression.

The Delivery of Podcasts

Chapter 9—Hosting the Podcast. This chapter explores several options for hosting your podcast files. Learn your options for delivering your files and ways to avoid expensive hosting charges.

Chapter 10—Creating the Feed. You podcast needs a RSS feed to list its contents. Search engines and podcast directories require this information in order to list your show. Learn what goes into the podcast feed and easy ways to create a compatible podcast.

Chapter 11—Publishing and Promoting the Feed. Learn how to submit your podcast feed to directories as well as which directories matter. This chapter will also offer expert advice on how to promote your show and give you a few ideas on how to monetize your program.

Harnessing the Medium

 Instead of putting a CD-ROM with this book, we've built a blog and podcast. Be sure to visit www.VidPodcaster.com. We'll keep the book up to date, share the latest news and developments, and offer useful video tips. There's also an area just for the reader's of the book. You'll find several files for each chapter available for download. To access the exclusive files see the ad at the back of the book.

The Icons Used in this Book

Gear Up—Recommendations for gear that makes the job easier or adds quality to the final production.

Further Reading—Recommended books or resources that let you explore a topic in greater depth.

To Watch—Recommend video sources that will aid in your understanding of podcasting.

Web Link—External websites that offer additional resources or information.

Noteworthy—Learn important "gotchas" or pitfalls that can put your production at risk.

Technical Tips—How-to's or important advice on how to get the job done.

Our Approach

Our advice is practical … we don't teach you how to cheat … we don't treat you like you are "dummies." Our productions vary; we've done work for Fortune 50 companies as well as small non-profit associations. We have been in front of the camera as well as behind it. We teach you how to produce podcasts that look professional while being keenly aware that podcasts are a price-sensitive commodity.

We will offer you multiple approaches that address high-end and budget conscious workflows. We are fully cross-platform and use Macs and PCs in our daily lives. We also use tools and gear from a variety of manufacturers. We'll offer our opinions, but feel that they are well-formed. We'll also offer options and differing points of view, as we know that you'll want few choices.

Our Qualifications

At the time of this publication, our company, RHED Pixel (www.RHEDPixel.com) will have produced close to 3000 podcasts. We've developed web video for companies like Microsoft, Apple, and Google. We've also worked with everyone from educators to professional speakers to fund-raisers. We've produced podcasts on a variety of topics, software training, emerging technology, digital photography, health, fitness, and science.

We have spent two years developing this book. Rather rush this book out the door; we have refined our workflows and opinions. The material in this book has been thoroughly tested. We have learned from years of video production and from working on so many podcasts. We live video and new media production every work day; the advice you'll find in this book is how we get the job done.

We'd like to think you'll find it useful. We've written and produced more than 25 books and DVDs that are used by media pros just like you. We believe in karma … we take the hard lessons we've learned and offer it back up to the industry as a whole.

We hope you enjoy and we invite you to become part of the conversation by joining us at www.VidPodcaster.com.

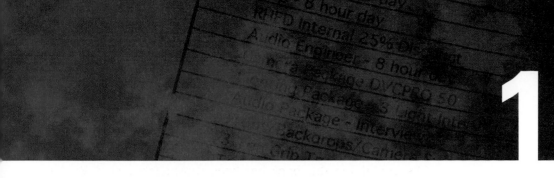

THE BUSINESS CASE FOR PODCASTING

There are several differing opinions on the importance of podcasting. The meaning of the term podcasting is often debated; some take a broader view that includes the use of streaming video and web players, while others adhere to a stricter definition of downloadable media using syndication technology. What most agree upon, though, is that the world of digital media is constantly changing.

Portable entertainment and education has gone truly portable with devices like the Apple iPhone

Podcasting is a symbol of that change. It is possible for a podcaster to reach out and connect with large audiences. These audiences may not rival those consuming mainstream media (although some podcasts regularly outperform cable and network television), but your chances of reaching a substantial percentage of a niche market is substantial. One thing is certain … the cost of reaching an audience through podcasting is dramatically less than it is through traditional distribution methods.

Consumers want video content. They are looking for news and entertainment that they can relate to … that addresses their needs and specific interests. Podcasting enables this sort of relationship. Whether you are a business, a trade association, a government agency, or even an enterprising individual, you can harness the power of podcasting to reach an audience. Additionally, the video you produce for podcasting is fully compatible with other video distribution channels, ensuring that you can repurpose your content to reach the broadest audience.

Understanding the Audience

Before we explore other aspects of podcasting, let's first address the makeup of the podcasting audience. By knowing who's watching, you can better understand the opportunities that podcasting presents. The podcast universe is diverse and constantly growing, meaning new opportunities continue to arise.

Podcasting Awareness

The good news is that podcasting awareness is growing. The bad news is it has aways to go. According to Edison Media Research and Arbitron, in the year 2007 one-third of people in the United States had heard of podcasting. While those numbers may seem low, the growth is still impressive. By comparison, in the year 2006, the awareness rate was only one out of five.

This growth in podcasting is largely tied to the rise in portable media players. Podcast support has been added to players manufactured by Apple, Microsoft, and Sony. Together these three

Portable Media Players Matter

 According to The Diffusion Group, 54% of podcasts are consumed on a portable device rather than a personal computer (www.tdgresearch.com).

manufacturers have at least 85% of the market (with reports as high as 75% for Apple-branded players). Many users looking to fill their media players with content turn to podcasting as it offers a source for diverse content.

Who's Watching

The podcasting audience is very diverse, but it skews younger. Half of all listeners are under 35. The flip side of this statistic is that half of the audience is over 35 ... which means that you can reach a wide variety of people. Let's take a look at the specific breakdown.

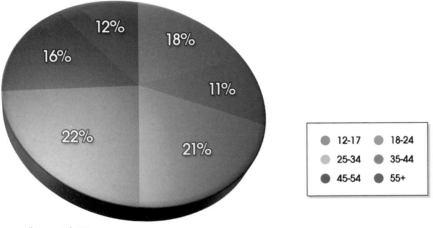

www.edisonresearch.com

Audience research has shown that 18- to 24-year-olds are more likely to download audio. Twenty-five- to thirty-four-year-olds are the biggest consumers of video. The popularity of video podcasting in older demographics is due in part to the need for faster Internet connections and more expensive hardware (both things that come easier to older, more affluent audiences).

What is important to note is that the podcast audience is pretty well diversified. For example, the same survey by Edison Media Research found that the podcast audience is 49% female and 51% male (essentially an even split). You'll need to make this a part of your business case when discussing podcasts with potential clients and industry peers. There are a lot of misconceptions about what podcasting is and who's watching ... your job is not only to make podcasts but also to help others understand in what situations podcasting works best.

Video Requires Active Viewing

Video podcasts require much more attention from the audience than an audio podcast. You can listen to talk radio in the background. With video, you have to more actively participate in consuming.

What's Holding Podcasting Back?

One of podcasting's limiting factors is the inertia new technology experiences in adoption. The mainstream population needs time to learn how new technology works and what it is good for. For example, TiVo-style DVR devices debuted in 1997 … and the media is only now reporting that the product is expected to be "mainstream" by 2010 (when it is estimated to be in 50% of all homes). For those of you counting … that's a 13-year journey.

Another of podcasting's limiting factors is its name. Many people are stuck on the word *podcast*, believing that they have to have an iPod if they want to consume podcasts. What is important is to emphasize the features of podcasting, rather than its name. Many consumers are interested in accessing video that is highly portable and easy to get. Content that speaks to their special interests, that can be subscribed to for convenience, and that can be delivered with little or no effort.

Consumer-controlled video is the future, and podcasting is on the forefront of that revolution. Over time, the market and technology will likely evolve. In order for a podcast (and podcasting as a whole) to succeed, it is essential to emphasize the benefits to the potential audience as well as enable the audience to consume podcasts in easier ways.

What's Happening: Growth and Trends

There's a lot going on with web video in recent years. Technology has continued to improve at a rapid pace, which has enabled both the growth of new audiences and new opportunities and the ability to deliver a better-looking product to these audiences. Many of the industry's largest television networks and video producers have also embraced web video as an opportunity to create additional revenue streams for their content. Podcasting is a piece of this new market, and one that many believe encapsulates the best opportunity to bring video to consumers.

The Growth of Broadband Internet

While podcasting and web video do not require broadband access, they certainly thrive with high-speed connections. Fortunately, broadband Internet access is finding its way to the masses. According to the Pew Internet Project's September 2007 survey, half of all Americans have broadband access at home. And broadband will continue to surge: The same survey found that 70% of users who had an Internet connection used broadband. While international access rates vary greatly, trends consistently show growth of broadband on a global scale.

The Fast Pace of Broadband Adoption

Broadband Internet access has hit the 50% adoption milestone faster than most other consumer technologies. It has taken about 10 years for broadband to reach 50% of adults in their homes. For example, it took 18 years for color TV to reach 50% of Americans, 18 years for the personal computer, 15 years for the cell phone, 14 years for the videocassette recorder, and 10.5 years for the compact disc player.

The Growth of Internet Video

The growth of broadband video has had an impact on the viewing habits of its users. The Pew Internet & American Life Project found that in the year 2007, "fifty-seven percent of online adults have used the internet to watch or download video, and 19% do so on a typical day." Broadband users are more likely to consume video; three-quarters of broadband users download video online.

This growth of podcasting is due in fact to the social aspect of online video. The same survey found that "half of online video viewers (57%) share links to the video they find with others, and three in four (75%) say they receive links to watch video that others have sent to them."

These trends bode well for the podcaster. If you produce high-quality video that is on-target, your audience will share it with others. This type of growth is often referred to as viral, and it works well online. Success can come much quicker than through other media outlets, at a lower cost since traditional advertising often has little to do with viral growth.

More on Viral Growth

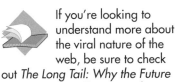

If you're looking to understand more about the viral nature of the web, be sure to check out *The Long Tail: Why the Future of Business is Selling Less of More*, by Chris Anderson.

Familiarity with Podcasting

 The Diffusion Group found that podcast awareness was performing well for the new technology. According to their 2007 study, they found that one-sixth of Americans identified themselves as having tried podcasts.

- Among US broadband users, 16% have listened to a podcast at some point, saying that they either have listened to a podcast but no longer do or that they currently use podcasting.
- 10.5% say that they currently use podcasting.

(www.tdgresearch.com)

The Involvement of Big Business

Podcasting is a part of traditional media's plan to stay relevant. Television networks in particular realize they need to move their video content to the web, enabling both space shifting and time shifting. The challenge here is that many of these traditional content generators hold on their "old ways of thinking." While these studios would benefit from podcasting, many want greater control over their digital files through the use of digital rights management (DRM) technology.

In 2007, Motorola found that 45% of European broadband users watch at least some television online. The percentage was as high as 59% in Spain and France. Entertainment insiders agree: A 2007 survey of television executives points to continued online video growth. Eighty percent of those polled said that at least 40%, if not a greater proportion, of video will be consumed on the Internet (rather than television) by the year 2012. Before you get too optimistic, only 26% of those respondents said that video content would be distributed freely. Rather they expect that content owners will mandate royalties.

Despite these conflicting goals, podcasting still stands a healthy chance at success. Many podcasts have successfully embraced non-intrusive advertising approaches, enabling the podcaster to promote interest in their program. For example, several TV shows use podcasts to further connect with their audiences. A good example is the Sci-Fi Channel, which offers a very large series of online videos and podcasts that build interest in the show.

What will continue to be a struggle will be meeting the demands of consumers while generating revenue for the content creators.

How to Explain Podcasting to Your Clients

While we'll explore the technical details of podcasting throughout the book, let's establish an easy to reference analogy that can be used with clients. We equate a podcast to a media tool that behaves like TiVo or a magazine. Both of these media forms allow people to choose topics that they are interested in, both offer subscription models, and both allow time shifting and space shifting.

With podcasts and TiVo, people can watch or listen at their convenience—not just when a program is broadcast. Both podcasts and TiVo let viewers browse and search; viewers can pick what they're interested in, and then watch it when it's convenient.

Many people browse and try things without ever subscribing. For example, you might find yourself at an airport with a little time to fill. You might walk up to a magazine stand and if a cover catches your interest you might try it. After reading the magazine you likely make a decision about its value. You'll choose not to

Letting your clients hold a podcast is a great way to illustrate the portable media concept.

Arbitron's Findings

Arbitron is a group that is frequently called upon to provide statistical research for radio stations.

- Eleven percent of all Americans have listened to podcasts. That translates into approximately 27 million Americans that have tried podcasts.
- More than half of all teens own an iPod or other portable media player.

read it again, to try it out when you think of it, or to subscribe. The idea with podcasting is similar to a magazine ... a show's long-term success is dependent on getting viewers to subscribe.

When to Use Podcasting

Podcasting is the right choice for many scenarios (but not all). We find that many clients want to consume a podcast but aren't fully aware of the commitment it entails. In order to be a good vendor, you must provide existing and prospective clients with the proper perspective on what's involved with podcasting.

Let's first take a look at some good reasons to use podcasting.

Compete in an Open Market

Podcasting is a relatively open market, which means that independently produced shows can do as well as those produced by major television studios. While ABC, CBS, and NBC can spend a fortune on promoting their podcasts, you'll find that independently produced shows are right next to them in rankings.

What makes it possible for independent shows to do this well is the democratic nature of podcasting. Podcast consumers want good content. While it helps to have a major network promoting things, if you can get a little bit of buzz on your own, you can succeed.

Players like the Microsoft Zune help extend podcasting's reach.

Grow an Audience

Podcasting can be used to successfully grow audiences for other products you may offer. Many book authors have podcasts, which help in exposing their books. The same holds true for professional speakers who want additional exposure. Even those without financial goals in mind can benefit. For example, several churches have begun to take their services or sermons and make them available. This allows people who can't attend (such as the sick or those traveling away from home) to stay in touch with their church and faith. If you already have an audience in a traditional medium, using a podcast can strengthen or build the connection.

© istockphoto

The delivery of traditional media can be a significant cost if you have a large audience to reach. A podcast can deliver video, audio, and printed information.

Save on Traditional Distribution Costs

Another benefit of podcasting is that it can help reduce traditional distribution costs. For example, a podcast can help minimize shipping, duplication, and mailing costs. Due to the subscription nature of podcasts, you can minimize the use of email blasts and promotion efforts that you would have to do to remind people that stuff is up online.

Podcasts can also replace other forms of traditional media. For example, anorganization could turn its printed newsletter into a podcast. Selected stories could be turned into an audio or video podcast, while the traditional newsletter could be included as a PDF file within the podcast. Podcasts offer an opportunity to translate old media to new media; this can offer new opportunities for cost savings and growth.

Brand Extension

Let's face it … there are a lot of similarities between most commercial products. For example, why choose one digital camera over another? Depending on whom you talk to, you can get a myriad of reasons … and that's where podcasting can come in. Through a podcast, a manufacturer can teach its product users and potential customers how to get more value.

Podcasting offers walk-away brand extension, the ability not just to promote a product, but also to show people how other people are using the product. The camera manufacturer could not just have engineers or product managers talking about the latest features. Rather, they should interview professional photographers talking about photo techniques as well as showcase amateur photographers and their photos. Sure, these people all likely use the camera manufacturer's gear (and they might mention it), but broadening the scope of the podcast will help it succeed. Let guests talk about other technology they use and things they like, right. Don't just limit a podcast so it becomes a marketing shill—otherwise, your audience will stop tuning in.

When Not to Use Podcasting

While podcasting is an amazing medium to communicate with, it is not the perfect tool for all scenarios. If you try to force a client into podcasting, you can create disappointment. Similarly, if a client comes to you wanting to create a podcast for the wrong reasons, you would be doing the client a disservice by not presenting options to them. It is always better to think of the long-term results over the short-term gain.

With this in mind, when might podcasting be the wrong choice?

Commitment Issues

At some point in your life, you likely wanted a cat or a dog for a pet. One of the objections you probably heard was that you had to be ready to make a commitment to its upbringing. Would you be ready to feed it, play with it, and clean up after it every day? While you can take a dog or a podcast for a walk, the similarities don't end there.

A podcast is a commitment. The podcaster needs to be prepared for ongoing costs for tasks like editing new episodes.

A podcast requires attention. You need to create new episodes and then add them to your podcast feed on a regular basis. You have to pay attention to what your viewers are saying about you. You have to think about adding new features to a show and making improvements to your graphics and production process.

A Useful Source of Podcasting Statistics

Are you looking for the latest information on podcasting and web video? Then be sure to check out Paul Colligan's blog at www.paulcolligan.com/podcast-statistics/

Blogs are Essential

A podcasts needs a blog to help it connect with an audience. Be sure your podcast has a strong web presence that lets viewers go deeper.

Having a podcast involves ongoing expenses. It takes human resources and financial resources. We're not saying you should continue pouring money into a sinking ship; we have launched and canceled podcasts, sometimes we refine and relaunch, sometimes we let the idea go. But you do need to realize that launching a podcast is a commitment. You also need to make sure that whoever is paying the bills is aware of this fact.

Savior Complex

People who want to "partner" and produce new shows approach us all the time. If a client comes to you with the idea that their podcast is going to attract all sorts of people and it's better than anything else out there, be a little cautious. We generally ask them "How else do you connect with your audience?" If they don't have anything else to offer, then their podcast may take several years to succeed (if it ever does).

We've learned that good talent and an interesting concept are not enough. A good show concept is important, but you need to have talent that is out actively speaking to the public and media. They need to be connecting with people through things like a blog, a magazine, or books.

A podcast will very rarely succeed on its own. It needs to be part of a coordinated effort to publish or extend a brand. A podcast alone does not make a brand except on the rarest occasions. Even podcast phenomena like *Ask a Ninja* have a blog with products available for sale, as well as press releases and other activities to reach out.

Make sure you measure your client's expectations. Don't sell them podcasting as the greatest thing ever. This will just create unmeetable expectations, which will cause frustration for all involved.

Performance Obsessed

The challenge with podcasting is that it is so new … this means that the metrics used to measure downloads and reach are still being refined. For example, a server can miscount downloads if someone starts to pull down a podcast, then interrupts the download (by shutting down the computer) and resumes later. Likewise, counting can be skewed because many measuring services look for unique IP addresses. For example, an entire computer lab or wireless network might be using a shared IP address, which means that 25 users might be counted as one user. With this said, you can still get fairly accurate statistics about downloads.

If your hosting company doesn't offer statistics (or you want an additional source) we recommend Podtrac (www.podtrac.com).

Podcasts can be tracked to give you a better idea of your audience.

With this service you insert a code into the tagging information for your podcast and the code triggers a counter for each episode. It is possible to get statistics on a per-country basis. You can see on what day the most episodes were downloaded and how long it took between when the podcast was released and when people became aware of it.

Instead of obsessing over the number of downloads or a show's ranking in iTunes, you would do better to keep an eye on trends. Is your show growing or shrinking? Are you seeing spikes on certain type of episodes when you change things? Do people like your guest host? Do some show's topics resonate better than others?

Results Obsessed

With any financial investment, it's reasonable to expect results. Many web ads posters focus on "click-throughs." Radio and newspaper advertisers often talk of "impressions." Well … what about podcasting? How do you measure an audience's response? When is a podcast generating results?

It's not that easy to get people to take immediate action. Marketing people often focus on building awareness or multiple impressions. Many people expect an instant response (like Pavlov's dogs when they heard bells). Sure your show can have ads in it, but it's difficult to track the effectiveness of ads. But this is true of most advertising models.

What many people don't want to hear is that coupons and codes don't usually work. Sure, you might see an ad in your local newspaper that advertises a new restaurant. The restaurant prints a coupon for a free appetizer and you go, "Oh that's a good coupon. I should go and try that restaurant." Chances are you'll forget the coupon or leave it in the car, but still end up at the restaurant. People just don't remember special codes or web URLs. They just don't. They hear about something. They don't remember where they heard about it, but they eventually take action because awareness builds.

© istockphoto

No iTunes?

 If you want to keep your show out of iTunes, you can. One way is to simply not register your show with their directory. You can find more about blocking your feed at www.apple.com/itunes/store/podcaststechspecs.html.

Privacy Concerns

Two things that many clients will be concerned about are spam regulations and the privacy of their audience. The good news about podcasting is that it is an opt-in audience. Nobody who gets your podcast can accuse you of spamming because they came to you willingly. Additionally, subscribers are not providing any personal information, so there are no records to protect, no credit card numbers to be stolen, no privacy issues at all from the consumer's point of view.

Security Concerns

Some clients may want to keep their podcast private. This can be a bit of a challenge—podcasts are designed to be shared. One solution is to place files on an internal network (such as an intranet). Then subscribers can only access the files when they are on the secure network. Another solution is to not register your feed with directory services; then it's like an unlisted phone number.

Clients may ask, though, "Can we make it secure so that if they put our podcast on their iPod or laptop and then lose it, somebody else can't watch it?"

"Well, both laptops and iPods have security features, like ,password screen locks. Then people would have to type in a code to access the files."

"Well that's too much of a pain …."

"No I'm sorry we can't account for carelessness. You can either train your people that the information is sensitive or not. This is a public format, so if you want secure things that don't leave the walls of your company, don't make it a portable file that can leave the walls of your company."

How Does It All Come Together?

Now that we've made a business case for podcasting, let's take a look at the experience of consuming podcasts. We regularly find that even the media savvy harbor several misperceptions about podcasting. In our next chapter, we'll explore in depth the podcasting consumption experience and offer a clear view of what the technology is and is not.

Adobe Media Player Allows for Rights Control

If you need a solution that allows for some levels of security or login, be sure to check out the Adobe Media Player. Adobe has stated that they will support more options that give content creators greater control over security and digital rights.

PRO*file*: **Culture Catch**

Culture Catch is a smart culture community that was launched in July 2005. Based in New York City, the company was founded by Richard Burns and Dusty Wright. While Culture Catch (www. CultureCatch.com) is a well-known podcast, the company also produces various live events that let their members interact. Over one million people regularly visit the CC website, attend its live events around the world, download its audio and video content, and engage with the community.

Culture Catch currently shoots two video podcasts per week. The show has conducted interviews with cultural notables like David Lynch, Wynton Marsalis, Laura Dern, Richard Branson, Duncan Sheik, Henry Rollins, Bob Costas, Les Paul, Russell Simmons, Donovan, Gore Vidal, and Kevin Bacon; all of these interviews are available on the site or on iTunes.

Wright and Burns were drawn to podcasting after trying to launch similar shows via traditional broadcasting venues.

"We got tired of all the gatekeepers in conventional media telling us that our show ideas were too smart, or too long, or expensive, or not the right fit," says Wright. "Podcasting is so liberating on so many levels. It's refreshing to meet so many different folks creating niche programming and really burning with the passion to produce it."

Burns adds that podcasting lets him focus on the creative aspects of filmmaking he enjoys so much.

"As a filmmaker, when a project ended so did your employment. I was spending 90% of my time looking for work or

money to create films and 10% creating films, which seemed very stupid," he explains. "As a podcaster, I spend 75% of my time creating and 25% on the business of podcasting. Much better ratio for an artist."

Podcasting has become a full-time job for Wright and Burns. The interest and sponsorship their show, website, and events have attracted let them focus solely on Culture Catch.

"This is my full-time gig and I love it," says Wright. "It has allowed me to streamline my productions, too. I think about our shoots like a field reporter. I carry just the bare essentials unless we're really looking for some serious production value and then we might bring in a third cameraperson. But normally we look at each interview situation and determine how we want to shoot it before we hit 'record.'"

Culture Catch regularly shoots with two cameras. This gives Burns more flexibility when he edits the podcasts. Both Wright and Burns fill multiple technical and creative roles during shoots.

"A low-budget production like a podcast requires the podcaster to wear all hats (or at least many)," says Burns. "In my case, that's audio, video, grip, director, editor, production manager, craft services, director of photography, makeup, etc. Thus, prepare and accept that you'll make some really stupid mistakes."

Wright tells us he learned the hard way about the importance of constantly checking for problems: "I once interviewed Daniel Lanois and didn't check my audio levels before I started the interview. I had a bad cable. I couldn't use any of it. I wasted one of the greatest interviews I've ever conducted. He talked about producing U2 and Dylan and Emmylou Harris. It makes me sick to think that I didn't take the extra few minutes to check things out."

Burns agrees. "Always check audio and picture before recording. What you see and hear on the camera monitor isn't always what you are recording."

Wright and Burns emphasize that being passionate is the key to succeeding at podcasting.

"Dare to be different. Dare to push the creative envelope," says Wright. "Don't let others tell you that you're wasting your time. If you feel your niche content can reach 60,000 other

© 2007 Susan J Weiand

like-minded individuals, then go for it. If you're looking to reach the masses, it's possible you might. Grab your camera and mic and go … you'll know soon enough if it's working or not. And if it's not, tweak it until it is."

"The industry needs more personal voices and experts," Burns adds. "Make your show very personal and niche. Big networks can't do that kind of programming. They are about broadcasting to a wide variety of people. Podcasting is about reaching a specific audience, owning the audience and developing a business model that services that audience."

Gear List

- Two Sony 950 3-CCD Mini DV cameras
- Two Sony EL 77B lavaliere microphones
- Four EV mics (one RE635, one RE50ND, two RE16s)
- Two Shure (Beta 58s) mics
- Three Element Labs LED lights (brilliant lights, don't get hot, don't burn out, can use a remote to program color correction, etc.)

WHAT PODCASTING IS
AND IS NOT

Video podcasting is relatively new … it's fairly complex … and it crosses several professional lines. Creating a video podcast requires skills of video production, web publishing, and project management. From the consumer's point of view, podcasts are somewhat tricky, not because they are hard, but rather because there are so many different products and companies that offer support for podcasts.

The vast majority of people are still confused about what a podcast is. They've heard the word, but if pressed to define podcasting, they'd likely say, "Well, you know, it's like stuff that you can download and watch." While that's a true statement … it's a bit too vague. It's like asking, "What's a zebra?" and getting the answer … "You know … it's like an animal." In order to create podcasts, you'll need a solid understanding of the technology.

17

Just What Is Podcasting?

 Many people refer to podcasting as *portable on demand casting*. It is thought of as an alternative to broadcasting. Podcasting offers portable content that people can watch when they want, on a variety of players.

The Clear Understanding of the Technology

Podcasting is another name for audio and video blogging (you may also hear the words *netcasting* or *videocasting* used by some). The general idea is that you post audio or video content that someone can subscribe to. You are essentially creating a channel, one that you add audio, video, or print content to so it can be automatically downloaded to a subscribers' computer or media player. All of this can occur without the need for e-mail blasts, people logging onto websites, or expensive shipping bills.

Additionally, podcasting is much more affordable than streaming and web video options. Podcasting uses a distributed model, so instead of everyone coming to your website and clicking (then wanting to watch the video at the same time), podcasts download in the background automatically. This means that podcasts are there, waiting to be watched whenever the consumer wants them.

Common Misperceptions about Podcasting

As a podcast producer, you may be called on to act as both an evangelist and a consultant. Not only will you have to give your clients a clear definition of podcasting, but you'll also need to debunk myths and misunderstandings.

Podcasting does not require an Apple iPod. Consumers can use all sorts of technology to consume podcasts, including laptops, televisions, or a Microsoft Zune (as seen here).

The biggest misunderstanding is that people ask for a podcast when all they want is a video file that will play on an iPod. That is not a podcast … it is an iPod-compatible file. Releasing a single video file does not make a podcast … at best; it's a webcast, a one-time sort of thing. The likely motivation here is that the client wants to do a press release saying they did a podcast or to report to their shareholders that they've launched a podcast.

So what is a podcast? There are a few criteria that must be met if you want your video to be considered a podcast.

1. **Highly Targeted Content.** The first is that the content should be highly targeted; that is to say, the content is intended for consumption by an interested audience. Podcasting is generally considered to be targeted at niche markets.

2. **Compatible Files.** Additionally, the content can be an audio, a video, or even a print file that is distributed via the Internet. The technology relies on relatively open standards like MP3 for audio, MPEG-4 for video, and PDF for print.

3. **Syndicated.** In order for a web video to be a podcast, it needs multiple occurrences. Those occurrences are serialized, which means there is some sort of plan for when they come out. It can be daily, weekly, monthly, or as needed. Consistency with your release schedule is important for building an audience.

4. **Subscription Option.** A key aspect of podcasting technology is its subscription component. Interested parties have the ability to subscribe to your podcast (and unsubscribe) at their own volition. The subscription part is what's really important and differentiates podcasts from other forms of web video.

This is the simplest definition that properly encapsulates all aspects of a podcast. All of these points need to be met if you want to create a podcast.

Is Podcasting Restrictive?

While there are some strict guidelines of what makes a "true" podcast, don't let this scare you away from the technology. Any video that you create to use in a podcast can also be released by other means. You can take podcasting content and post it to video-sharing sites like YouTube; you can take any of the video files and embed them on a web page; you can even put the video on traditional channels like DVD or broadcast.

Devices like Apple TV and TiVo allow for podcasts to be viewed on television sets.

The Birth of Podcasting

Podcasting is a direct descendant of blogging (which we'll explore in detail later in the book). In 2003, the blogging community wanted the ability to expand their blogs and looked to add audio and video files to their blogs. The core technology of blogs is Really Simple Syndication (RSS), which allows content to be cataloged and makes subscriptions possible.

The drivers of RSS modified it so that enclosures (like audio or video) could be attached. This opened up the option to add MP3 audio, MPEG-4 video, or PDF files. Essentially, podcasting was born. So the technology has been in place since about 2003, but the term wasn't used in print until August of 2004.

Where does Apple fit into all of this? Apple did not invent podcasting. Nor does podcasting require Apple hardware or software. But Apple is responsible for making podcasting broadly available and popular. Apple embracing podcasting and making it a part of their hardware and software brought podcasting to the masses. Others have followed suit, including notable technology companies like Sony and Microsoft.

The beauty of podcasting is in how it gives the consumer access to great content. Podcasts are easy to browse, share, and transport. Podcasts also work on many different playback devices from many manufacturers. So while podcasts are a bit restrictive in their requirements, they open up significantly once they are published.

Technology Choices

The growth of podcasting is tied closely to the technology that drives it. This is not to say that bad content can succeed (after all, unwatchably bad content is still unwatchable). But podcasting offers an audience options that make watching your programs convenient. In this day and age, there is no shortage of content, but making good content easier to acquire and consume increases the likelihood it will be watched. Podcasting technology ensures that finding and downloading programs is easy, and that the files are broadly compatible with several playback devices.

Using a Podcast Aggregator

In order to make podcasts easier to find and consume, most people choose to use a podcast aggregator. An aggregator can be a stand-alone software application or a website. Consumers use podcast aggregators to browse podcasts that they are interested in. The podcasts can then be subscribed to for consumption of future episodes.

Websites like podango.com allow users to browse their library of video podcasts.
Users can subscribe at the site or click a single button to subscribe using their aggregator
of choice.

An aggregator automates their process of checking for new content. The users specify how often their aggregator should check for new content: check every five minutes, check every hour, check once a day, and so on. Once new content is found, the user can also specify what should happen. An aggregator can download everything that's new, download the latest episode, or simply inform the user that new content is available.

If a user wants to consume video podcasts, a broadband Internet connection is very desirable. While a podcast can be consumed over dial-up, dial-up is a very slow way to pull down large files. There are podcasting software solutions for Windows, Mac, and Linux users.

Aggregators can also be content-management systems. For example, users can manage their podcasts using Apple's iTunes or Microsoft's Zune software. They can choose which episodes to sync with their portable players as well as how to handle old content (such as automatically deleting previously watched episodes to save hard drive space). Let's take a look at some of the leading software aggregators for video podcasts.

Not All Web Videos are Podcasts

In order for a web video to be a podcast, it needs multiple occurrences. Those occurrences are serialized, which means there is some sort of plan for when they come out. It can be daily, weekly, monthly, or as needed. Additionally, a podcast needs to offer a subscription component that can be joined or left at the end user's discretion.

Apple iTunes

Apple's iTunes (www.apple.com/itunes) is the number one cross-platform solution for podcasts. It began its life as a simple MP3 player, first introduced in January 2001 at the MacWorld Expo (nearly a year before the iPod was revealed). The player has evolved into handling everything from music and audio books to Internet radio and podcasts. The application also ties directly into the iTunes Store, which is the number one marketplace for both digital music and podcasts.

The iTunes application is available as a free download. It works on Mac OS X, Windows XP, and Windows Vista. Many people install the application for its integration with Apple's iPod and iPhone product lines. Still, people choose to use it on its own for its flexibility and convenience.

With version 4.9 of iTunes, released in June 2005, Apple added support for podcasting. Users could choose to manually enter an RSS feed to subscribe to a podcast or they could browse the iTunes Store. Apple's podcast directory in the iTunes Store is the largest available, and most podcasts see the bulk of their subscriptions coming from this source.

Sony Media Manager for PSP

While the Sony PlayStation Portable (PSP) (www.sony creativesoftware.com) is thought of first and foremost as a gaming system, it has several options for playing back video assets. Sony enabled content to be viewed via UMD discs, but only commercially produced titles are available this way. To allow for broader content, Sony enabled podcasts to be transferred to the device. Additionally, the PSP includes a wireless Internet connection and a web browser. These tools allow the PSP to actually subscribe to podcasts and have them download directly to the device.

Microsoft Zune Marketplace

The Microsoft Zune player (www.zune.net) is designed to be an alternative to Apple's iPod. As such, it has a few features that were not standard on the iPod line, such as an FM tuner and a web connection. Over time, these features were added to the iPod. At its original launch though, the Zune lacked what other portable media players had: support for video podcasts.

In late 2007, Microsoft updated the Zune player line, as well as their software and marketplace. Support for MPEG-4 video is now native (previously, video podcasts had to be converted to a Windows-only format).

The store has a much smaller collection of podcasts to choose from (launching with just 1000 podcasts at its start). But over time new shows have been added. Podcasters can suggest their own shows to the Zune editorial team through a link on the podcast home page.

Adobe Media Player

The Adobe Media Player (www.adobe.com) is an evolution in podcast aggregators. The tool was designed from the ground up to enable end users to view Flash video content in more convenient ways (including offline viewing). In late 2007, Flash evolved to be able to play H.264 encoded video as well. This significantly broadened the capabilities of the Adobe Media Player which launched in the Spring of 2008.

The program offers fairly standard features similar to those of other podcasting aggregators, including the ability to catalog and search for shows. The Adobe Media Player supports RSS, which allows subscriptions and automatic download of content.

Where the player becomes unique is in its customization. The player offers advertising or branding space, which allows graphical content to be preloaded into the player. New graphics can also be dynamically loaded. This opens up options for both internal uses for corporations and broader advertising solutions. The player also supports significantly more powerful measurement tools that can offer statistics to the podcaster about viewership habits and consumption.

Miro Podcast Player

The Miro podcast player (www.getmiro.com) evolved from a previous product called the Democracy Player. The player software is unique in its broad support for platforms. Besides supporting Windows and Mac, the software runs on several versions of Linux, including Ubuntu and Fedora.

Miro is well suited for several types of online video because it can play MPEG, QuickTime, AVI, H.264, Divx, Windows Media, and Flash video. The software is

The Columbia House Records Effect

There is a resistance among users to click the subscribe buttons on podcast pages. We call this the Columbia House Records effect. "Surely it can't really be free. Even though it says free subscription … I must have to enter some sort of personal data or you're going to secretly charge my credit card somehow."

This resistance leads to the viewer deciding that they'll just return on a regular basis and click download. Unfortunately this doesn't work; people get busy, they forget, etc. Over time, your audience numbers will go flat (or even decline).

What you really want is for people to subscribe; that's what you're pushing for. As such, emphasize the subscription option through the show and in the podcast description. You need to convert casual viewers into subscribers. To do so, you'll need to earn their trust.

an open source project, which means it has been developed by several programmers in an open-access model, as defined by the Open Source Initiative (www.opensource.org).

Like other podcatching software, Miro supports the use of playlists and RSS subscriptions. You can also group your content and organize your shows, setting them to expire if you want to manage your hard drive usage. The tool is quite elegant and offers an open source option to those who shy away from the larger manufacturers. Most importantly, Miro is the link that brings podcasting to other platforms besides Mac and Windows. The software has also been localized to more than 40 languages, which makes it a popular tool outside of the English-speaking world.

Subscribing versus Downloading versus Streaming

There are several ways for your audience to consume a podcast. A video podcast is an MPEG-4 video file, which is one of the most universally compatible video formats on the market. This flexibility is at the core of podcasting, in that it gives your audience options.

- **Subscribe.** The subscription component of podcasting is what makes it unique and truly useful. For the consumer, subscribing ensures that the content is ready to watch whenever they want it (including situations like traveling where an Internet connection might not be present). The subscription component also helps a podcaster grow their audience over time because it makes retaining viewers easier.

- **Download.** While a podcast subscription will also download files, what we mean here is the traditional download model. Many podcast consumers are used to traditional web video, a model that requires visits to a website. Many podcast consumers will visit a web page to choose the files they want, and then download them for later consumption. While this approach is valid, you will want to educate this portion of your audience and train them to become subscribers (which offers a greater long-term benefit to both parties).

- **Stream.** Many podcasters have embraced streaming players. This allows the podcast to be shared via blogs and social media sites. While these players are not true podcasts, they are a compatible technology. In fact, Flash is often the choice for these embedded players, and Flash video has evolved to be podcast-compatible. In 2008, Adobe enabled Flash video and its Adobe Media Player to handle H.264 video files (a common podcasting format). The streaming option is popular because it lets a potential podcast consumer try out your show. This option is not limited to Flash, though. Many consumers will "audition" podcasts within iTunes, clicking to load the files for viewing without ever subscribing or downloading. This all ties into consumer behavior, which is often based on "try before you buy" (or in this case … before you commit).

How to Subscribe to a Podcast

Most consumers utilize a podcast aggregator program. This can automate the process of checking and downloading. Most modern web browsers support RSS feeds as well, which means the podcast feed can be bookmarked. While new episodes won't download, your browser will indicate the number of unread (or unviewed) items in parenthesis.

Portable Players

The focus in podcasting is often the portable aspect of the media files. Portability has two meanings: the ability to transfer from one device to another with ease and the ability to use playback devices that can be easily carried. There are several portable media players on the market, but not all support standard video podcasting formats.

Apple iPod and iPhone

The best-known podcast player are the Apple iPods. While it had fairly basic features at its launch in 2001, the iPod has continued to evolve with major improvements. For video iPod podcasters, the iPod line added support in the fifth-generation models for video playback in 2005. Another leap forward came in 2007 when

Is an iPod or iTunes Required?

A common misperception is that Apple hardware and software is required. This is just not the case. While Apple makes several very popular solutions, they are not the only option for podcast consumption.

video playback was extended to the lower-priced iPod nano. This is an important change, as it brought the option of portable media players with full-color video to a broader audience.

Apple has experienced great success with its multimedia phone device called the iPhone. By combining the powerful features of an iPod, cell phone, digital camera, and e-mail and web browser into a hand-held device, Apple connected with the market. The iPhone is also fully capable of syncing video podcasts from the user's library and opening up playback options in several mobile environments.

Microsoft Zune

After partnering with several portable media manufacturers, Microsoft surprised many with the announcement of their own portable media player, the Zune. The first Zune player was released in November 2006, and the product line saw major revisions one year later. Currently comprised of three models, the Zune has fully embraced video podcasting.

The Zune offers support for unprotected .WMV, MPEG-4, and H.264 files; the latter two are what matter most to podcasters. The Zune offers a wireless connection that continues to evolve and add new options for syncing and sharing.

Sony PlayStation Portable

For many, the Sony PlayStation Portable (PSP) is an attractive option. First released in 2004, the device is targeted to those who like video games but want a bit more in their portable player. Unlike most other players, the PSP uses a wide-screen aspect ratio.

The PSP supports RSS feeds. These allow the user to download video web feeds or watch podcasts from websites. If users want to save podcast content, they can write the files to the Memory Stick Duo (a proprietary format used by Sony). Additionally podcasts can be synced from a user's computer. Older PSP units may need to be upgraded, but this is easy to do, as the units can download free software updates directly from a wireless network.

Creative Zen and SanDisk

The other two companies known for making portable media players are SanDisk and Creative Zen. While these players are popular and offer several models and price points, they aren't a perfect fit. Their products support audio podcasts through MP3 files, but broad support for MPEG-4 formatted video has not been implemented. At best, these products require re-encoding video podcasts to a new format and lots of extra effort by the end user.

Other Players

It may sound obvious, but podcasting is not just about portable media players. There are several devices with broad support for podcasts. By enabling video content to be delivered to a wide variety of devices, podcasting has grown in popularity with both consumers and podcasters.

Desktop Computers

The vast majority of video podcasts are consumed on personal computers. People are interested in the content, and watch it right away. Most users are also using desktop computers to store and manage their digital libraries of photos, music, and videos ... so it is a natural fit that podcasts are a part of this library.

When you add to the fact that computers are very prevalent in workplace and education environments, it is a natural fit that users would seek the little escape that podcasting can provide.

Laptop Computers

Podcasts are very effective for corporate audiences. Many businesses use podcasting as a way to stay in touch with their remote workforce. That same workforce also finds itself traveling, so portable news and entertainment is often desirable (after all, how many times can you watch Beast Master on late-night cable TV?).

A laptop is an excellent podcast player. Most laptops can easily get on the Internet via a wireless or wired connection. Laptops generally have good screens and sound systems (people claim the laptop is for work, but it makes a pretty good DVD and gaming system as well). A laptop is also capable of running on a battery, ensuring that its owner can easily access content.

TiVo DVR

A popular make of digital video recorders is TiVo. These boxes are very popular among consumers, as they allow for the recording of television programs, which can then be watched at a later time. To broaden the appeal of the devices, TiVo has implemented support for podcasting on three fronts.

The first way is that a select number of programs are available as TiVoCasts. These are essentially podcasts that are released at a large size and are intended for playback on the set-top boxes. These shows can be visually browsed and recorded for viewing like any other program on TiVo. In order to work, you'll need a TiVo Series 2 or later DVR and a home network.

Podcast versus Broadcast

Like television programs, a podcast can cover any subject or genre. The key difference is that podcasts can come from anywhere in the world. Because they are downloaded, you can also watch them whenever you want.

Chances are that your program is not already listed in the TiVoCast directory, which means that a user has to manually subscribe. The second method is a little difficult, as the consumer has to use a remote control to enter the RSS feed. This process is not hard; it just requires that your audience have an exact URL for the feed. You can publish this address and instructions to your show's website.

The third way that TiVos support podcasting is through the TiVoToGo software option. This software enables you to connect a TiVo to PCs on a network in order to share audio and video files. This option is acceptable, but not as seamless as the two previous options.

Apple TV

Apple released the Apple TV device in 2007 as a way for users to synchronize the contents of their iTunes library with their home entertainment centers. The Apple TV device can browse up to five computers on the same network that give it permission, as well as sync its hard drive with one computer. The sync method allows faster playback of content without tying up the network. Apple TV is a digital media receiver than can interface with Mac OS X or Windows running iTunes. Apple released a major update in February 2008 which allowed for the browsing of podcasts without using a computer. This direct browsing method will make it even easier for people to browse and discover shows.

The implications for podcasters is that any content down-loaded by their audiences can be easily integrated into a home entertainment center. In fact, the Apple TV devices opened up support for HD podcasts, because the hardware is designed to both stream and playback video in the 720p format (video captured as 1080i can be easily converted). The device has already seen updates, including the ability to play YouTube content via streaming. Future updates should unlock broader support for video podcasts.

The Road Ahead

Now that you understand both the business case behind podcasting and the technology that powers it, let's move forward. We will now explore the production process to create video podcasts as well as the technical requirements for delivery. Along the way, we will revisit several of the points made in these first two chapters in greater detail.

3

PREPRODUCTION

Success Doesn't Just Happen

There's one thing we've learned in our years of making video—without a plan, you're likely to fail. Despite this hard reality, many people often do everything they can to avoid preproduction. Most creative types would rather get their hands on a video camera or a nonlinear edit system than sit down and do paperwork, budgeting, or risk analysis.

We're right there with you … we enjoy the act of creation as well. But proper preproduction brings an increased likelihood of financial and professional success … two things that are needed if you'd like to survive in the world of video production. In this chapter, we'll focus on practical advice and techniques that are easy to implement.

Making the Go/No Go Decision

When we discuss podcasting with our clients and potential clients, it often involves a reality check. Due to the popularity of podcasting, many people and organizations want to do it. But wanting a podcast and being able to support it are two very different things. To put it another way, just because you like kids or puppies doesn't mean you're ready to raise one.

Letting your client hold a podcast in their hand helps them understand the power of portable media.

After all, a podcast is a commitment … it takes time. In fact, the puppy analogy isn't too far off … you have to raise it, house it, feed it, and monitor it. A lot of clients just aren't prepared for the costs and time commitment required to keep a podcast running. Whether you are working with internal clients at your organization or external clients coming to your company for production services, be sure to educate them regarding the efforts needed to maintain a successful podcast. Selling a client something they aren't prepared to use is just bad business.

Creative Development

A key step in your show's preproduction is creative development. The show's concept needs to be developed beaten up, chewed up, and then spit out. Chances are your original ideas and assumptions will be a lot stronger after you put them through a creative wringer. Here are a few things we've learned in developing new shows.

1. **Don't try to reinvent what already exists.** You need to closely examine what's already in the podcast universe. Don't waste your time developing a concept that is identical to a hit show. After all, it's a rare day when the clone surpasses the original. With that said, don't give up on your idea, refine it.

There are podcasts on nearly every topic imaginable (this is a snapshot of the Health category in the iTunes Store). Be sure to do a little market research on your topic and explore your competition.

2. **Figure out what you can do differently.** If your competition offers long shows, offer shorter shows to appeal to those on the go. If your competition comes out monthly, come out weekly. If the competition takes a serious approach, look at humor. In other words, don't change the subject, do change the delivery. In broadcasting, it's called counter-programming and the concept holds true here as well.

Some categories, such as comedy, are very competitive. Take a look at popular shows and their descriptions and keywords. This can help you identify your target audience.

The Five W's

While it may seem a little cliché, another way to refine your show's concept is to ask the standard who, what, where, when, and why questions.

Who—Who is going to watch the show? Who is going to host the show?

What—What topics will the show cover? What genre or format will it use?

Where—Where will the show be recorded? A studio? On location?

When—When will the show come out? Weekly? Monthly?

Why—Why would a viewer subscribe to the show? Why would they come back for another episode?

3. **Decide who you want to attract.** Podcasting is a niche medium. Going after a smaller, targeted group is what it's all about. You need to think long and hard about who you want to reach. By refining your audience, you stand a much better chance of appealing to them and capturing them as subscribers. That's not to say you want black-haired, blue-eyed, left-handed, 27-year-old chemical engineers. But a podcast that goes after engineers of all types would probably fail just as badly. What's important here is that you identify a specific group with specific interests, then develop content that fits their needs.

4. **Make sure your visuals matter.** Could your podcast be delivered as an audio-only podcast? If so, don't create a video podcast just to make a video podcast. Video podcasts often have smaller markets than audio podcasts because they require more hardware to play and take longer to download. Additionally, video podcasts cost more to produce, edit, and deliver.

Video podcasts are becoming rapidly available to the masses with players like the iPod nano making portable media players broadly affordable.

5. **Determine the hardware capabilities of your audience.** You need to make some assumptions about your audience. Will they view your show on portable media players, laptops, or set-top boxes? Do they want faster download times, or are they willing to wait for a high-definition (HD) episode to download? You need to give careful thought to how your show will be consumed if you want to avoid alienating prospective viewers.

Determining Production Needs

The greatest challenge in creating a good podcast is the planning it takes to get the show out of the "big idea" stage and into production. Podcasts are amorphous; you'll face several challenges as you try to pin down what a show is about and how to pull it off. Matters are made worse by the relatively level playing field. After all, producing a hit show is within the reach of a first-time podcaster. Combine this anticipation with the mandate to succeed that clients often demand, and you've got a giant hairball.

Our advice is simple: divide and conquer. No, we're not talking about barbarian hordes or cellular reproduction. Rather we mean good old project management. The easiest way to determine how to produce your show is to divide it into smaller parts. We often find that a podcast series is easier to plan for when we first take the time to identify all of the elements that are going into it. For

Tip: Double the Size, Quadruple the Rest

Many video podcasters are embracing larger video podcast sizes. While the 320 × 240 size is well suited for portable players like iPods, those viewing on laptops and televisions prefer the image clarity offered by larger sizes. But what's the impact of using a 640 × 480 podcast?

- File sizes are approximately four times larger.
- Download times are approximately four times longer.
- Hosting and delivery costs are approximately four times greater.

Don't be discouraged, just be sure that you can afford to give people what they want and that they are willing to wait for that larger size. Some podcasters take the "easy" way out and offer both sizes. This strategy can work against you though as your show's ranking on the iTunes charts can be negatively impacted as each version is tracked separately.

example, let's take a look at a potential new video podcast we are developing to teach Microsoft PowerPoint.

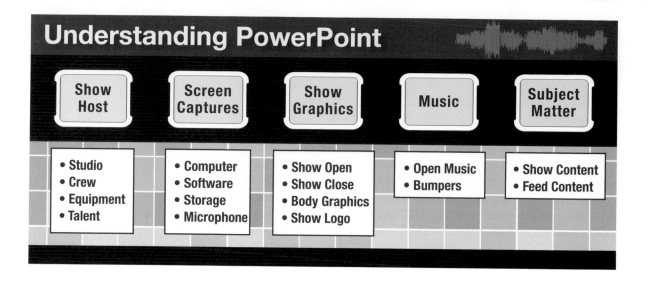

In this case, there are five general things an audience member will experience. These include

- A show host who keeps the viewer interested and gives the show its personality.
- The screen captures that show the software application being used.
- Show graphics that provide brand identity.
- Music that helps create mood and pacing.
- Compelling subject matter that must be developed through scripting or outlining.

As you can see in the figure, each element needed can be further refined into a more detailed list of ingredients or tangible items. By continuing to identify and specify, you can eventually develop an accurate list of requirements and items that will allow you to develop a budget.

This process of dividing a project into smaller pieces is called a work breakdown structure or WBS. A WBS analysis works well for both budgeting and project planning. Another way to approach it is to consider what you would do if you had to cook a ten-course meal … how much would it cost? How would you plan for it? The first step would be to identify what the ten courses were. Next you would identify the ingredients for the ten courses. This would

Scoping the Project

Developing an accurate scope statement is essential if you are producing podcasts for hire or as a service. Scoping is the act of saying, "Okay, we need to make a podcast … what does that mean?" The scoping document goes beyond the work breakdown structure and can serve as a basic agreement or an attachment to a standard legal contract.

It generally takes between 2 and 16 hours to scope a project, depending on the complexity of the project. We have never regretted making a scoping document, only not making one.

Essentially you are trying to identify what work is being performed, who is going to do the work, and when the work will be considered done properly. For example, "we will launch a podcast" is a nice statement. "We will produce and launch a video podcast with one episode released on a weekly basis; during production x number of episodes will be shot over two consecutive days with each episode having a run time of five to seven minutes each. A single graphical identity will be developed for the show and inserted into each episode. The show will be listed in seven directories." is a much more specific statement.

A scoping document generally runs between 2 and 10 pages and it becomes a charter for the project. In a way, it can become the basis of a contract in the future. You will want to get all project participants to attend or you want to have multiple phone conversations and then present it for review. Here are a few more tips to help you make a better scoping document:

- Avoid adjectives at all cost. You are being hired to produce a podcast, not a great, successful, compelling, invigorating podcast because those are completely subjective. If you put adjectives into your contract you are inviting legal debate over whether or not you successfully delivered what you promised. Do not put adjectives into any of your documents that describe the statement of work. You can put adjectives in your bio. You can put adjectives in customer quotes. But don't put adjectives in the statement of work.

- To save you from having to reinvent the wheel, we have made our scoping document template available to you at www.VidPodcaster.com (just see the Chapter 3 tab). First you name the project, then offer a short summary about the project. The template asks you to give a little bit of background information and a couple of bullet points on why this project is being done. Then you fill in a list of deliverables, a rough schedule with major milestones, and a budget.

- Simply putting these key points into writing can eliminate several conflicts early on. Things like the "actual" deadline come out and the "real" decision makers are identified. We always list the client's name directly, with a signature line for approvals. By requesting a signature on the scoping document, you will find out who really has approval authority for the project.

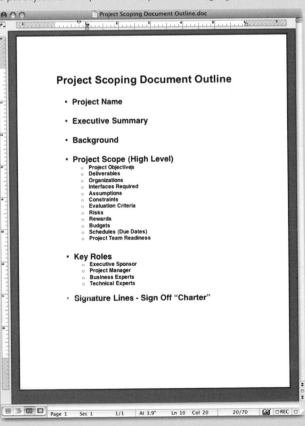

Budgeting Templates

 Looking for an easy-to-use budget template for your video podcasts? You can download a spreadsheet to use with Microsoft Excel or Apple Numbers from the Chapter 3 tab on the book's website.

Shot Ratio Matters

Between DV tape and FireWire hard drives, the concept of shot ratio seems to have gotten lost. With podcasting, your shot ratio matters. For those who need a reminder, shot ratio is the ratio of how much footage is acquired versus what's used in the finished cut. For example, if you shot 60 minutes of material and used 20 minutes, that would be a 3:1 shot ratio. If your shot ratio creeps above 4:1, you need to closely examine your shooting and production style. The only exception is multi-camera style productions. In this case, just count how much footage was used from the most utilized camera to produce the finished piece.

give you a much better idea of what that ten-course meal would cost and how long it would take to prepare. The work breakdown structure is relatively simple to use and implement ... we *strongly* recommend making it part of your budgeting process.

Budgeting Guidelines

If you're looking for a pot of gold, you're chasing the wrong leprechaun. Podcasting budgets are not the same as feature films or commercial spots. With podcasting, the key to making money is efficiency. Figuring out how to do more with less is the guiding principal. In this section, we explore practices that affect the bottom line.

Don't Make Assumptions

With podcasting, you need your shoots to run smoothly and efficiently. You will not be able to get the most out of your shoots if you've based your preproduction on bad information. You really want to know the goal of the shoot, the objectives of the shoot, how many podcasts you are trying to accomplish, and that the client, the talent, and the director have the same expectations. We have found that we can record up to 30 podcasts in a day if we plan properly and the talent is prepared. The bottom line here is efficiency. Be efficient, have a plan, and execute the plan with the minimum number of resources, and you'll do all right.

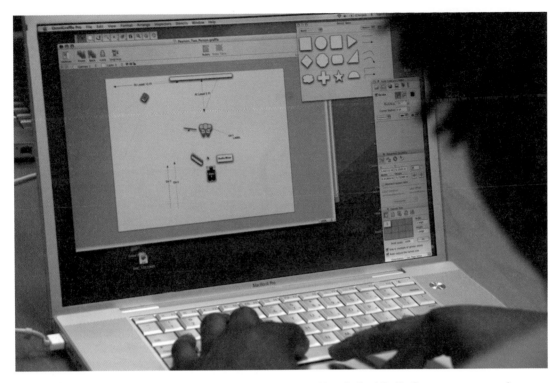

Creating a set diagram is a helpful way to plan for a shoot. Being used here is Omni Graffle Pro, an easy to use software tool for Macs.

How the Federal Government Estimates Time

There is a formula that many project managers use that comes from federal contracting practices: $(1*O + 4*M + 1*P) \div 6$. That's 1 times an optimistic time work estimate, plus four times a most likely estimate, plus one pessimistic estimate, then divided by 6.

Here's how it works. Go to a member of your project team who's going to work on the task (such as the editor) and say, "So, how long would this take?" Note, this is not the most likely number. This is the optimistic number, because if you ask any creative person how long something is going to take, it's an exaggerated number based on their ego and personal value, which is always high (this is not a slam on creative types, it is just true).

Then you ask, "Well if it was anybody else doing the work, how long would it take?" This is the most likely number.

Next you ask "If things went wrong that we really didn't count on, computer problems, bad communication, what's a bad case scenario?"

Then you do the math: one times the optimistic work estimate, plus four times the most likely estimate, plus one times the pessimistic, divided by 6. This gives you a more accurate time estimate for the work at hand. You can increase the accuracy by surveying other subject-matter experts (such as all the editors in your office).

This how the government does averaging, but you have to do it at the work package level. By getting the subject-matter experts involved, you are more likely to get accurate numbers about the work to be performed.

Keep It Short

Here's a simple idea: Keep your podcasts short. It is better to have eight 5-minute episodes than one 40-minute episode. We try to keep our video podcasts to less than 10 minutes. Audio podcasts can go up to about an hour because listening is a more passive experience. You can listen to an audio podcast while driving (please don't watch a video podcast while driving, it's a bad idea).

Remember that your audience is often watching podcasts "on the go." Be sure to keep your run times shorter to cater to your audience's needs.

Video podcasts tend to be consumed during things like work breaks, downtime, and airplane flights. Others will use them during commutes on the morning train or the subway. Think of podcasts as portable, on-demand learning or entertainment.

In the training podcasts we produce, we generally try to limit topics to one per episode. And if a single topic takes more than 10 minutes to explain, then we'll split the podcast into two or three parts. This way the viewer can download Part 1 and start watching it while they're waiting for the rest to download or be released. There's nothing wrong with multiple parts. That's the whole concept of serializing a podcast.

Treat Podcasts Like an ENG Style Shoot

Most podcasts are unlikely to have huge budgets. It's a good idea to design your podcasts using the principles of Electronic News Gathering (also known as Electronic Field Production, EFP). The guiding principles here are speed and agility in acquiring the footage as well as swiftness in editing. The primary concern is getting the material to the audience in a timely fashion.

News-style production is known for its efficiency, yet retains production values that are perfectly acceptable to most television viewers. You should strongly consider adopting this approach when planning your podcasts.

Look to Maximize Day/Schedule

Podcasting is a subscription-based service, which means you have to have more than one show to push out there. You've got to have episode 2 … you've got to have episode 15 … you've got to have episode 50 to really make podcasting viable. We generally build our days around a 10-hour schedule, which leaves about 7 hours of time for shooting and the other 3 for setup, breaks, and teardown.

We try to maximize the day, not kill the crew … there's a difference. Maximizing the day means allowing time for a lunch break. It means doing your best not to let the client schedule the first interview for 8:00 a.m. We've often had to convey to the client, "If you schedule this for 8:00 a.m., it means we have to leave our houses at 4:30 a.m. in order to have to set everything up."

Don't Share Line-Item Budgets

Although using a line-item budget is essential to creating an accurate budget, we try hard not to share these outside the company. We do not give clients line-item budgets because it often leads to unnecessary quibbling. Instead, we "roll" the budgets up. Identifying the major work packages to be performed and the total cost per category (such as preproduction, production, and postproduction). For example, we say, "The project management fee is this and it includes the following items."

Remember, even "basic" setups take time. Don't underestimate your call time for shoots.

Lessons Learned

A big part of budgeting is time estimation (how long will this take me to do?) One of the best sources of information is to look at time records from earlier projects. Learn from your mistakes by looking at your past budgets and time logs.

We routinely have to remind clients that an eight-hour day does not mean eight hours of interviews. We also have to point out that it is a contiguous eight hours. You can't schedule a crew to start at 9:00 a.m., then give them a four hour break in the middle of the day, and want them tape something that goes until 10:00 at night.

Be sure to work with your clients and gently educate them. Sometimes we've had to say, "Yes, we can do this. But we're going to have two crews and we're going to have a changeover period here and the second crew will step on to the set and continue into the night." Be smart: Respect your clients and your crew if you want the best results.

Try to Piggyback

If you have a client who is doing video production distributed by more traditional methods who is thinking about trying podcasting then consider piggybacking a podcasting shoot on top of a regularly scheduled shoot. The difference between the cost of paying a crew for a 10-hour day and an 8-hour day is often very minimal. Just be sure to discuss the 10-hour day when you book the crew. You can then get a few sample episodes in the can while utilizing your existing setups.

Maximize Locations

Every time you move equipment, you will lose at least 30 minutes (if not more). Our solution is to look for locations that can easily provide multiple shooting opportunities. When selecting a practical location, we try for one where small changes in the camera placement or framing result in a new look. If we are creating a set, we often just change the color of the backdrop, which can quickly result in a new look. You want to minimize crew movement unless it is essential.

Consider Spending Money to Save Money

While it may seem counter-intuitive, spending money on crew and the right equipment can save you money in the long run. We're not talking about a craft services table with lobster bisque

If you try to run with a "one-man-band" approach, you'll likely miss critical action. Be sure to staff appropriately for your shoots.

The Risks of a One Man Band

One-person crews are very risky, trust us we've tried. For example, if you have a one-person crew and the crew has to go to the bathroom, your gear is at risk. If you have a one-person crew and that person gets sick or injured, the shoot is over. If you have a one-person crew and you have to fly somewhere, you've got $600 in baggage overages (which could have paid for another crew person).

Our general approach is this: We try to use a three-person crew. We send two people from our office and hire one person locally. The local person will usually show up with things like lights and grip gear (which is affordable to rent) and our crew shows up with audio and camera equipment.

and imported beer, rather having the right gear and a multi-talented crew. The mantra of "fix it in post" should rarely be heard on a podcasting set. We have found that relying on the "fix it later" philosophy can consume up to three or four times the cost of taking the time to make adjustments during field production.

The guiding principle here is that you never want to miss an opportunity to capture content because you didn't have the right gear or crew. This may sound contradictory to the ENG comments made earlier, but it's not. What we are emphasizing is the need to balance the size of your crew and equipment so they are fully utilized without being pushed to the point of breaking.

Proper Crew Size

For most podcasts we've produced, our budgets allowed for crews as large as five. The flip side is that we've had podcasts where we've done it all with a crew of one (and if it were possible, the client would have requested the robotic camera). Our podcast crews usually include two or three media professionals (we try to have one more crew person than we do cameras on set). Depending on the style of video projects you normally work on, this size crew may strike you as normal or woefully understaffed. What it really comes down to is having the right people and equipment in the field. Multi-talented crews are essential; you will need individuals that are comfortable shooting, lighting, and recording audio.

Instead of saving money by cutting crew, look at your travel options and try to find airlines with liberal baggage allowance policies. We usually use JetBlue (reasonable excess baggage fees) and Southwest (three checked bags), which have the best baggage policies and flexibility for schedule changes. By cutting costs on travel, we can usually preserve crew size (and hence quality and sanity).

Multi-Camera Productions

It is becoming increasingly common to shoot podcasts with two or three cameras. This is largely in part to make post-production tasks like editing significantly easier. Many nonlinear editing systems, including those by Adobe, Apple, Avid, and Sony, now offer multi-camera editing. By shooting a podcast from multiple angles in real time, you have options during the edit. This works especially well for subjects like concerts, theatrical performances, hosted interviews, and how-to demonstrations. We'll explore this style of productions in more detail through the book.

Tapeless Acquisition

We have found that shooting direct to disk can be a big time-saver. This can be as simple as adding a special hard drive unit to your FireWire-based camera or switching to new formats like Sony's XDCAM or Panasonic's P2. Shooting tapeless can save time on the postproduction side. It also allows instant, in-the-field playback of a take. We often use it as a way to quickly drop a shot into a nonlinear editing application so we can check audio levels or try a color grading or compositing task.

Units such as this FireStore allow for a DV camera to record to tape and hard drive at the same time. These save a lot of postproduction time.

Selecting and Prepping Talent

Selecting good talent for a podcast is perhaps the most important thing you can do. It involves finding someone who can connect with the target audience and deliver a message while keeping them entertained. We've already spoken about the democratic nature of podcasting, which means the talent pool is a lot wider than it is for broadcast television. Podcasting audiences seem to prefer "regular" people as opposed to Barbie and Ken dolls, which often plague the airwaves. If you browse the top podcasts in each category on iTunes, you'll find a large assortment of "non-professional" talent and hosts.

Oftentimes, podcasting talent has little or no on-camera experience, which is okay if you properly prepare them. Make sure your talent is well rehearsed. Utilize the setup time prior to the

shoot to do an onset rehearsal. A lot of producers make the mistake of having the talent come only a few minutes before the call time. While the crew is getting set up we often ask the talent to show up and we just go have breakfast and we talk through things and let them get all their fears and anxieties out in the open.

Mapping the Production

It's a very good idea to determine your rollout plan early on. Remember, podcasts are serialized, which means that there is some sort of plan for when they come out, daily, weekly, monthly, bi-monthly, bi-weekly, on an emergency basis as needed, when inspiration hits … whatever it is. It is important that you determine what the schedule is going to be and that the client agrees. The frequency of release is one of the greatest impacts on financial cost. Be certain you've mapped out how frequently the show will be released. Similarly, be sure to gently remind the client to produce more episodes before the current crop runs out.

Choosing a Style of Production

Different styles of production can greatly impact the cost of your project. Be sure you identify how the podcast will be

Be sure to discuss a show's frequency and style early on with the client. These two factors affect the budget greatly and it's important all parties know what they are committing to.

acquired. Using a studio can drive costs down as it adds an element of control to the production process. On the other hand, screencast style productions for technical training often just feature the voice of the talent and a capture of what they were doing on their computer. Be sure to pick the best format to capture the visuals in your show that your budget can afford.

Picking an Acquisition Format

Choosing the right acquisition format involves balancing several factors. You need to examine the equipment you already own and measure against the benefits of new formats. This is an issue we explore more deeply in Chapter 5.

We have encountered a lot of production companies and clients who are obsessed about doing podcasts in HD. Our response is "Why?" We don't immediately discount shooting in HD, but we do caution against it if there is no compelling reason. If you or your clients want to shoot in HD, consider these issues:

- **A High-Definition Platform.** First, you should have some other purpose for the acquired footage, such as it will be distributed via Apple TV and TiVo HD or that you are selling the content in HD to a network.
- **Increased Download Times.** Are your consumers really willing to wait up to eight times longer for the files to download? Are you prepared to pay more to host those files?
- **Future Proof.** Does the content need to be preserved for an HD future? In other words, is the subject matter timeless or significant enough that there is value in spending the extra money to ensure that the footage can be used in an HD workflow for future projects or delivery?

Be sure to consider all uses for the video you acquire. There may be a secondary use or an additional market for your video, which will need higher image quality.

The vast majority of video podcasts are being delivered at either 640 × 480 or 320 × 240 pixels. For content that is mostly interviews or "talking heads," we usually choose 320 × 240. When the visuals matter more (such as technical training content), we choose the larger 640 × 480 delivery size.

PRO *file*: PhotoshopUser TV

PhotoshopUser TV (www.photoshopusertv.com) is a very popular podcast produced by the National Association of Photoshop Professionals (NAPP). The show offers a collection of tips, tricks, tutorials, and news about Adobe Photoshop. The show is published weekly, and has a huge following, keeping it consistently in the top five for its category.

The show is hosted by three well-known authors and trainers, known as "The Photoshop Guys." Each week, Scott Kelby, Dave Cross, and Matt Kloskowski get together to share time-saving techniques, inspirational photography, and technical news. The show is known for its mix of technical subject matter and humor.

"Just because you get in front of a camera doesn't mean you have to be serious," says Kloskowski. "If you are serious, then by all means don't try to change that. If you're not serious, then have fun. People can get the information in podcasts anywhere. They'll watch your podcast because of personality. They can relate to it."

This approach doesn't appeal to all viewers, Kloskowski acknowledges. He emphasizes that it is impossible to create a show for everyone.

"The sure way to failure is trying to please everyone out there. Pick an audience and stick with them," he says. "Cover the things that you're interested in. You'll enjoy it more and your audience will relate to you more if you do. For better or worse, put yourself, your opinions, your recommendations, and your personality into it and that's what people will come back for."

This approach has worked well for the show. PhotoshopUser TV frequently tops a million viewers for each episode. These numbers have attracted major sponsors to the show, which helps cover the cost of producing and delivering the weekly episodes. Viewers are encouraged to subscribe to the show so it will download automatically for them. Casual browsers can't access the back catalog.

"Every week, we post a new episode of PhotoshopUser TV that you can watch, download, and keep forever and ever," says Kelby. "We've archived previous episodes and you can download them for $1.99 per show. But members of NAPP have access to

the entire archive of PhotoshopUser TV episodes as part of their membership."

The charge for back episodes helps cover the cost of production and delivery. The decision to keep the shows free to members of NAPP increases the value of membership, which in turn attracts new members to the organization. The podcast also serves to publicize the books and magazines NAPP publishes, their online training program, and their conferences.

"We love to teach people how to use Photoshop, and podcasting was a way to get that training out to a lot of people that wouldn't have otherwise seen it. If they like it, then hey … good for them. They got some free tutorials and maybe

they'll come back and try our other products," said Kloskowski. "If they didn't like it then no harm done. It didn't cost them a thing. It really comes down to exposure though."

Their exposure plan has worked out well. According to Scott Kelby, "The show has reached nearly three million downloads in a month. We never dreamed it would take on the life it has, but we're thrilled to be along for the ride." The show is very popular on a global scale, and tops the charts in the International iTunes directories as well.

"It's amazing. We get emails, feedback, and questions from people around the world. It takes up a lot of time but it's fun, too," says Kloskowski. "I guess the main impact is time. It takes plenty of time to keep up with it, but the rewards (both business and personal) … are priceless."

Gear List

- Two Panasonic AG-HVX200 cameras
- Sennheiser wireless microphones
- Mackie Onyx Mixing board
- Altman floodlights
- Lowell Pro-lights, V-lights, and Omni lights
- Kessler Crane system
- Manfrotto tripods with 503 heads

PRODUCTION:
LIGHTING AND SOUND

Podcasts usually fail in two areas of production: The audio quality is substandard and the lighting negatively impacts the quality of visuals. The reason this occurs is that podcast budgets are often limited and thus crew sizes are constrained, so the gaffer and audio engineer are often the first positions cut from the crew. With this in mind, the podcaster must pay special attention to these two areas and develop the essential technical skills needed to create a professional production.

Great productions need great lighting and great sound.

Lighting on a Deadline and Budget

When it comes to podcasts, you will usually face constraints of both time and budget. Our solution is to work in more of an electronic news gathering (ENG) style of production while striving to achieve the results of a fully crewed production. In other words, how can we go in the field with a one- or two-person crew and successfully get what we need? This style of production is foreign to many video production professionals, but it is essential to podcasting success.

Because the size of your crew will be constrained, you need to have a crew that is multi-talented. This means that a crew of two or three needs to be able to do the audio, lighting, and videography, and often conduct interviews. A crew really needs to be able to be flexible to make podcasting viable in terms of the budget numbers. With this in mind, let's explore some specific lighting scenarios.

Lighting Considerations: Indoors

You generally have greater control lighting an indoor shoot, whether it be on location or in a studio, than you do for an outdoor shoot. The primary advantage you'll have lighting indoors is the ability to control both the amount and quality of light on your set. The various lights and accessories in your lighting kit will enable you to control the look of your shots through creative lighting design. Entire books and courses have been devoted to the color theory of light, but for our purposes let's take a look at the essential decision-making process.

1. What Is the Lighting Situation on Your Set?

Does your room have mixed lighting, such as sunlight from windows combined with overhead fluorescent lighting? Or is the light coming from a single source? Your first consideration should be to assess what kind of light is present on your set.

2. Can You Control the Color Temperature on Your Set?

Ideally, there is no natural light coming from windows or skylights. Additionally, you'll have the ability to control the practical lights present in the room. If this is the case, then the room is easier to light with the lighting fixtures in your kit. However, if you are in a room with windows, or lights that can't be shut off, then you will need to identify the light present.

3. What Is the Color Temperature on Your Set?

Light essentially has a visible color, and this is particularly true on camera. Think of a bright blue, sunny day or the warm, orange glow of a candle. In a basic sense, light takes on the following colors.

- Sunlight = Blue light
- Standard light bulbs (tungsten) = Orange light
- Fluorescents = Greenish light

4. Which Corrective Action Should You Take?

Once you know what light is present, you'll know what light to add to fix the room. For example, if you are in a room with large windows and you have tungsten fixtures, you'll need to take some corrective action.

Safety First

It is important that you be safety conscious with your equipment on your shoot. This means taking extra measures like using sandbags to secure lights as well as addressing cables. We highly recommend using rubber mats or taping down all of your cables. Make sure the whole area is safe, because the last thing you want is someone tripping over your production gear and suing you. You can also pack a small set of safety cones (often available from sporting goods stores) to help mark out your equipment.

You may need to use colored gels on your lights to change their color temperature.

One option is to cover all of the windows with a special gel called CTO (color temperature orange). This can be very effective, but is time intensive and expensive. The other choice would be to place blue gel on your lights. Gelling the lights is probably the best decision when time and budget are tight. However, keep in mind that full blue gel substantially reduces the intensity of your lighting fixtures, so you'll need stronger lights. It is for this reason you should use specialized fluorescent lights that can take both tungsten and daylight bulbs (more on this later).

5. Do You Have Enough Power?

When lighting indoors, be mindful of the amount of power that your lights are drawing. Let's keep it simple and look at a typical scenario for the United States. A standard current is 120 volts and most single circuits are rated at 15 amps. If we remember basic physics watts = amps x volts, so $15 \times 120 = 1800$. Therefore, a single circuit should be able to run at least 1500 watts of lighting before the circuit breaker trips.

But your lights may not be the only things drawing power on the circuit—it is usually impossible to tell how many outlets there are on a single circuit. Therefore, it makes sense to run several heavy-duty extension cords (often called stingers) from multiple outlets in the hope that you are spreading your power load over multiple circuits. Many older buildings have different wiring setups, and you should always check to make sure you don't overload a circuit, which could potentially be a fire hazard. Be sure you know where the electrical panel is so you can reset circuits as needed. After all, if a breaker is going to trip, it will usually wait until everything is set and you start to record your first shot.

Lighting Considerations: Outdoors

Whereas shooting indoors allows you a certain level of lighting control, the only certainty about shooting outdoors is that it will bring challenges. Besides the difficulty of inclement weather, you have a very unpredictable lighting source. Among the challenges you will be presented with when shooting outdoors are:

- Your light source is constantly moving.
- The color temperature of sunlight shifts throughout the day—remember to white balance your camera often.
- The light can change from hard direct light that casts strong shadows to even flat light and back again—all in a matter of seconds.

To counteract these curveballs Mother Nature might throw at you, you can make use of two kinds of specialty equipment.

Don't Use Auto White Balance

While you may be tempted to rely on an auto white balance feature on your camera, don't. The auto white balance can be overly sensitive to things like a passing cloud. Instead, just keep an eye on your monitor or viewfinder while shooting.

Large reflectors can be used to bounce the sun onto your subjects.

Reflectors

Unfortunately you can't change the position of the sun. But if you are dealing with direct sunlight you can use a reflector to redirect sunlight onto your subject and/or background. A reflector can be something as simple as a piece of white poster board, or a specialized, expandable piece of fabric such as those made by Flexfill. You should invest in a few basic reflectors for your own lighting kit.

HMI Lights

HMI lights are highly efficient and specialized fixtures. They can produce light with exactly the same color temperature as daylight. A 200-watt HMI can produce light as intense as that of a 1200-watt tungsten fixture (without needing nearly as much power).

There are two downsides to HMI lights for podcast production. The first is that they require a ballast to work (which is essentially an external power converter). This ballast contributes to the bulk of transporting these somewhat fragile fixtures. The second is their cost. A single 800-watt HMI fixture can cost in excess of $5000, and replacement bulbs run around $250 each.

We typically rent HMI lights from local lighting houses, thus eliminating the need to transport them over long distances. The typical rental fee for an 800-watt HMI is $100 to $200 per day. On the positive side, you usually have an abundance of free light when shooting outdoors.

Fixing it in Post?

While we are big proponents of getting it right in the field, we are also realists. Sometimes corners will have to be cut in the field in order to accomplish the shot or stay on schedule. Knowing what can be done in an edit suite is helpful so the director or DP can make judgment calls. It is often easy to tweak a slightly underexposed shot or increase the midtones to help separate the talent from the background.

Additionally, tools like Magic Bullet can be used to further enhance the look of the video during postproduction. Don't let your shoot deteriorate to utter crud, but be sure to know what you can and can't do with color correction. We try to light a podcast as right as possible, but if it means two lighting people and an extra $4000 worth of lights for a week, we'll sometimes make quality judgments. We recommend taking a test shot onto a laptop while in the field so you can fully understand the options you'll have with your footage.

Lighting Considerations: Multi-Camera

It is becoming increasingly common to shoot podcasts with multiple cameras (a technique we'll explore more in the next chapter). This is a common solution because it can both speed up the acquisition stage (by eliminating the need for multiple takes) and accelerate editing (by simplifying syncing issues).

Multi-camera shoots likely happen indoors … if not, they happen outdoors. Since we've already touched on both … what's different you ask? It's important to design lighting setups that provide even lighting for all talent without having the lighting stands in the camera's field of view. While this may sound easy, it gets much trickier to place lights when you have to accommodate multiple cameras. The most common approach is to hang the lights from a ceiling or a lighting grid. Since this may not be available, you'll need to think closely when positioning your lights.

Lighting Considerations: Available Light

Sometimes, you will have no control over lighting at all (such as at a concert or theater performance). In this case, you need to make do with what's there and properly set your cameras. It is a good idea to do a site survey before the job. Go and look at the location and attempt to see it with the lights set. You can then make better decisions about how to handle the lighting, such as go as is, or push to add more lights to the budget.

This concert by the Brindley Brothers was recorded at Jammin Java (www. jamminjava.com) using available light.

Recommended Lighting Instruments

The type of lights you choose to use on your podcasts will vary greatly depending on the style of production and your budget. When we build our lighting kits, we focus on performance, value, and flexibility. We frequently produce our podcasts in the field; as such we need lights that are durable, perform well, and are easy to transport. With this in mind, here are a few recommendations.

Tungsten Lighting Kit

One of the first investments video pros make is in a good tungsten light kit. The most popular manufacturers of these kits are Arri, Mole Richardson, Lowell, and LTM (among others).

Tungsten lights are mainstays in professional video production.

A standard kit usually includes three or four lights as well as stands, barn doors, scrims, and a travel case.

You can often find professional lighting dealers locally, or of course shop online. While the brand names of the contents will vary, you generally want to get a kit that contains lights of different types and sizes.

- A good kit will include an open face type light that can be fixed with a soft box to provide a broad light source and which is often used as a key light (especially when shooting interviews). This light will usually be rated for a 500 to 1000 watt lamp.
- The kit should also include several Fresnel lamps of varying intensity. Fresnel lamps contain a lens that allows you to control the spread of light from a spot to flood coverage. These versatile lights can be used to help fill in light on your subject, provide backlight for separation of foreground and background, and light elements of the background or set.

Other items in our Tungsten kit include:

- **Dimmers**—Dimmers control intensity of the lights with a slider or dial.
- **Gels**—These include a variety of color correction gels, theatrical gels in multiple colors for creating dramatic lighting environments, along with pieces of diffusion and neutral density.
- **Leather work gloves**—Tungsten lamps tend to get rather hot; don't get burned.
- **Blackwrap**—This is essentially heavy-duty aluminum foil that is coated black. It is used to wrap lights and prevent unintended light spills.

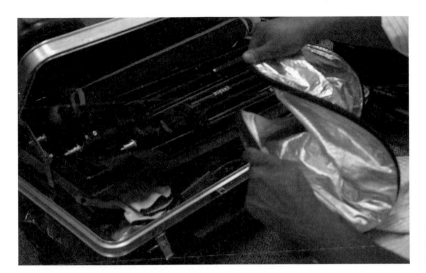

Make sure your light kit includes reflectors. These are very useful for both indoor and outdoor shoots.

- **Wooden clothes pins and gaffer tape**—These are used to hold gels and other lighting accessories in place.

A kit will generally cost between $1000 and $4000 depending on the features needed. When ordering, be sure to pick up spare bulbs since they break and wear out with usage.

QP Cards Make for Easy Color Matching

One essential piece of lighting equipment emits no light at all. We adhere a QP card on our clapboard. These adhesive cards are a small strip with white, neutral gray, and black. They are generally sold as a three pack for around $12.

You take one out at the start of your shoot and stick it on your clapboard. This way every take will have a color reference strip. Then in your editing software, you utilize a three-way color corrector with a white, gray, and black eyedropper. This makes it very easy to calibrate your camera angles in post and ensure accurate color balance.

Fluorescent Fixtures

The use of portable fluorescent lighting fixtures has become very popular among video professionals. Companies such as Lowell, Mole Richardson, and Kino Flo make these fixtures. The reason for their popularity is that these lights offer several great features:

- They are a great source of even, soft light that is ideal for shooting interviews or lighting a chroma key backdrop.
- They run very cool, allowing them to be easily moved. They can run all day in a small room without turning it into an oven. This is important to keeping your talent and crew comfortable.
- Many of the lights are modular, meaning that you can change the number of bulbs used in the fixture. They can also be equipped with either daylight- or tungsten-balanced lamps. This is a great time-saver during setup because you don't have to gel the windows. The lights are essentially two setups in one fixture. We know that we walk into any shoot environment, change bulbs, and turn the lights up or dim them down. It truly is a flexible lighting system.
- Many of the light control features such as barn doors and dimmers are built directly into some models.

Bulbs can be easily changed in this Kino Flo light.

- Many manufacturers offer kits that come with airline-ready shipping cases. They also meet the weight requirements of airlines, which make them easy to travel with. Speaking of travel, you can also find universal models that can be used anywhere in the world, switching from 90VAC to 265VAC.

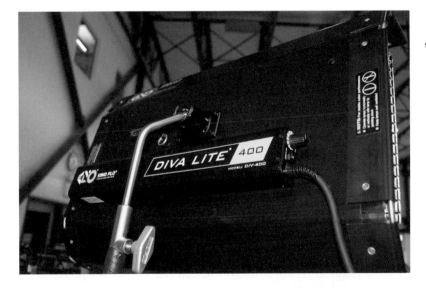

The light kits can be found starting around $750 for a single light kit and up to $3000 for multiple light kits with stands. While this is an investment, the lights have very much proven their value over time for our productions.

Refillable Sandbags

 If you go on any professional video set, you'll see sandbags in use as a protective measure to secure light and audio stands. But traveling with 250 pounds of sandbags can get expensive (and heavy). Instead, try refillable sandbags, which travel light. When you get to your location you can fill them with sand, rocks, or whatever else can be found nearby. A popular model by Lindcraft is made of durable Cordura Nylon with a heavy-duty zipper with a hook-and-loop cover flap to keep it shut. www.lindcraft. com/product_details/RS.html

China Ball Lanterns

On the opposite end of the price scale are China Ball lanterns. These are an easy and affordable way to illuminate a large area. The China Ball is a soft paper lantern that can attach to a light socket unit. The fixture can create soft natural light that produces pleasing skin tones.

While prices will vary, we often purchase ours from a website called Filmtools (www.filmtools.com). A kit needs the following items:

- **Paper Lantern.** These range in size from 12 to 30 inches. Cost is usually $3 to $20, depending on the size.
- **Practical Light Socket Assembly.** This is generally a medium socket with an on/off switch. The socket can handle up to 660 watts and terminates with a standard household connector. It costs approximately $6 per unit.

China Ball lanterns produce soft, even lighting that is affordable.

- **Lightbulbs.** Bulbs will range between $5 and $20 for photo-quality bulbs. Be sure you do not exceed the recommended wattage of the fixture.

These fixtures are very affordable, costing less than $50 each, and are also very easy to travel with. Just be careful that you monitor their usage. Because the lanterns are made of paper (flammable), you should not leave them unsupervised on the set.

Lighting Diagrams

To move the chapter from theory to practice, let's take a look at two common setups. These diagrams show you the lighting setups for several of the podcasts we have recently produced. Look closely at the lighting diagram as well as the photos to see the results. We've also included a lighting equipment list for each setup.

More on Lighting?

 There are several excellent books and DVDs that focus on lighting techniques for video. Here are a few we recommend.

Lighting for Digital Video & Television by John Jackman
Motion Picture and Video Lighting by Blain Brown
Video Shooter: Storytelling with DV, HD, and HDV Cameras by Barry Braverman
Light It Right by Victor Milt and VASST

Two-Person Interview

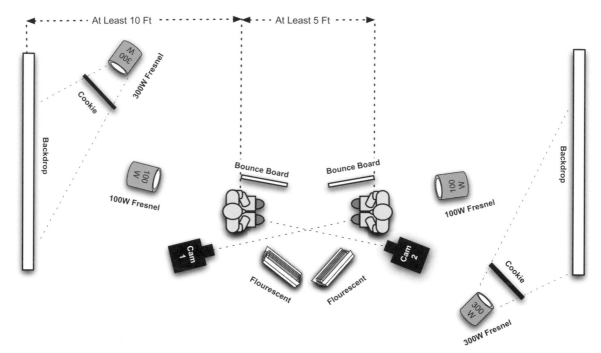

2	300-watt Fresnel w/ Barn door	1	Leather Gloves
2	100-watt Fresnel w/ 2 Barn doors	6	C Stands with Arms
8	Light Stands	2	10-lb Sandbag
1	Mathews Grip Head	2	Six-Port Power Strips
2	Reflector Holder	3	10-foot Three-Port Extension Cord
1	Gel and Diffusion Jelly Roll	2	25-Foot Extension Cord
4	300-watt Dimmers	4	Backdrop Support Bar
4	Ground Wire Killers	8	Medium Steel Spring Clamp
2	Tungsten/Daylight Reflector	2	Muslin Backdrops
1	Spare Lightbulb Kit	2	Kino Flo 200—2-Bank Kit
1	Gaffers Tape Roll		w/ Stands and Bulbs
1	Blackwrap Roll	2	White Card Stock (Bounce Card)

Technical Training Set: One Person

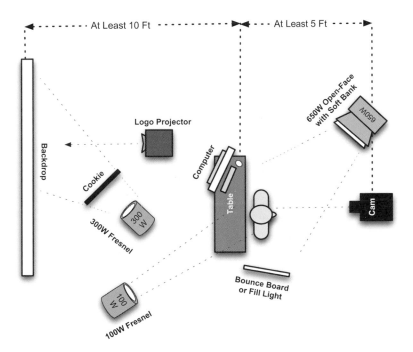

1	650-watt Fresnel	2	White Card Stock (Bounce Card)
1	Chimera Soft Box – Small – Speed Ring	6	C Stands with Arms
1	300-watt Fresnel w/ Barn door	2	10 Lb Sandbag
1	100-watt Fresnel w/ 2 Barn doors	2	Six-Port Power Strips
4	Lighting Stands	3	10-Foot Three Port Extension Cord
1	Gel and Diffusion Jelly Roll	2	25-Foot Extension Cord
4	300-watt Dimmers	1	Backdrop Support Bar
4	Ground Wire Killers	1	Overhead Projector
1	Tungsten/Daylight reflector	1	Client Logo Gobo
1	Lightbulb Box	8	Medium Steel Spring Clamp
1	Kino Flow 400-1 Bank	2	Muslin Backdrops

Three-point Lighting

Three-point lighting is the standard when it comes to lighting for film, video, or photography. This basic method, like the name implies, utilizes three light sources focused on the subject from different angles.

Key Light. The key is your primary light source. Generally this is your most intense light and it is placed between 15 and 45 degrees to the side of your subject. Using a broad soft source of light like that produced by a softbox or fluorescent fixture such as a Kino-Flo is ideal when shooting interviews.

Fill Light. The fill is your secondary light. It is placed opposite the key, and its primary function is to fill in the shadows cast by the key light. To what degree you utilize your fill light is a matter of creative judgment. Ideally you would use a smaller fixture as your fill light. but if your fill is the same size as your key you can lessen its intensity by

1. Increasing the distance between the fill and your subject.
2. Using a dimmer.

3. Placing additional diffusion in front of your fill.
4. Bouncing your fill light off a reflector or bounce board.

Backlight. The backlight is your third and typically least intense light source. Its purpose is to highlight the edges of your subject, thus separating the subject from the background, which creates a three-dimensional look. Placement of the backlight is usually behind and above your subject.

The Final Result. All three lights are combined.

Once you understand the principles of three-point lighting you are well on your way to understanding the art of lighting.

Capturing Good Audio

Recording clean high-quality audio is essential in podcasting. With a video podcast if your audio is poor you may as well have no podcast. If you dispute this statement try this: next time you are watching TV turn down the audio and see how much of your favorite program you understand. Then turn the audio up and close your eyes. You will most likely understand much more when you can hear what is happening versus when you can only see what is happening.

When shooting video people have a tendency to spend the entire effort focusing on the images and leave little time or resources dedicated to ensuring good audio is recorded. This is a mistake that many come to regret once they start the editing process. Despite how good your podcast looks, in the end if your audio is bad the whole podcast will come off as amateurish and fail to retain the subscribers you worked so hard to attract. Also keep in mind that since many podcasts are consumed on devices like the iPod where earphones are used, good audio is a must.

Essential Equipment

Odds are that the camera you are using to-record your podcast has a built-in microphone. While using the onboard camera mic works well when you are shooting run-and-gun style in the field; the audio quality of what you are recording is most likely poor. This is due largely to the quality of the microphone and the distance of the mic from the audio source.

When recording podcasts, you should use one or more professional-quality microphones. One thing you will need to understand about professional mics is that different types of microphones have different pickup patterns or directionality.

That is, the area from which the mic is designed to record varies depending on the type of microphone you use.

Mics that have an "omnidirectional" pattern pick up sound from all directions, and those that are "unidirectional" pick up sound from a specific direction. Unidirectional microphones are subcategorized based on their specific pickup pattern: cardioid (narrow), supercardioid (very narrow), and hypercardioid (extremely narrow).

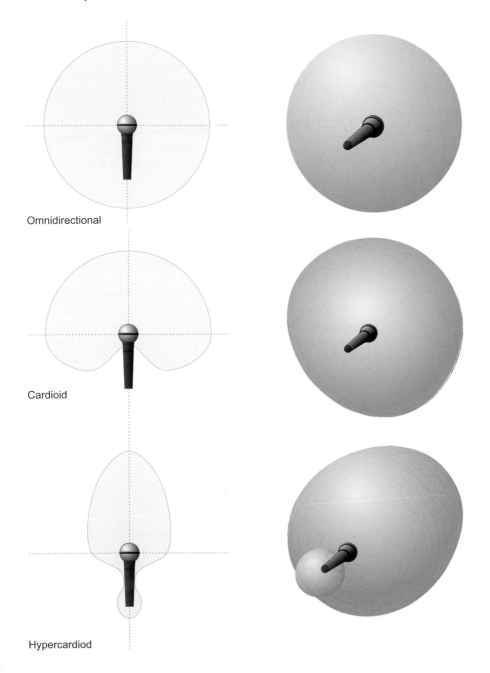

Omnidirectional

Cardioid

Hypercardiod

Lavalier

A lavalier microphone (or lav) is the small microphone you often see attached to the lapel, tie, or blouse of news anchors. These small microphones are ideal for recording audio from a single individual during an interview or a presentation. The pickup pattern of a lav is generally omnidirectional, but since it is placed so close to the speaker's mouth nominal background noise will generally be unnoticed once the levels are set on the recording device.

If you are using a lav mic and the interviewee is to be seated or is stationary during the taping, then running a cable (or hard wire) from the lav to the mixer or camera doesn't present a problem. However, if you are taping a presenter who is moving around, you will want to attach your lav to a wireless transmitter. This will convert the audio signal into radio waves on a specific frequency that are then received by a receiver attached either to the mixer or directly to the camera.

Using wireless mics can be very convenient for your talent but a good wireless system is often quite expensive (starting at $600). Additionally, you need to be cognizant of interference from a variety of sources if you decide to use them.

When attaching a lav mic you will want to keep a few things in mind:

- Place the mic about 12 inches below the person's mouth and try to keep the mic as close to the center of the body as possible.
- If you are going to try to hide the microphone inside of the person's clothing you will need to do it so that the mic does not rub against the person's body or clothes. This is quite tricky and usually requires some practice and the use of some strategically placed gaffer tape. Be sure to listen closely when monitoring the audio to ensure you are not recording rubbing sounds.

- Even if you are not concerned about hiding the mic, you should be sure to run the cable inside of the person's jacket or shirt so there is no unsightly cord running down the talent's chest when you switch to wide shot.
- When possible you should recommend that your talent wear a shirt with at least some buttons or a jacket. Trying to find a place to attach a lav to someone wearing a simple T-shirt always presents a challenge.

Shotgun

Shotgun microphones are typically attached to either a camera or a boom/fishpole. A shotgun mic is ideal when a talent is moving while talking. The pickup pattern of a shotgun mic is unidirectional and ranges from cardioid to hypercardioid, depending on the specific model of the microphone.

Although a shotgun mic can be used for recording stationary interviews, it is most useful when carried by a boom operator who positions the microphone as close to the talent as possible while

keeping it just outside the camera's frame. While this sounds simple, it requires a person with good coordination who can focus on the action and withstand the physical challenges of holding an extended pole above the talent for long periods of time. Often shotguns are used instead of or in conjunction with a lav mic during stationary interviews. Ideally you would use a stand with a boom holder in these situations.

Other things to keep in mind when using a shotgun mic include:

- While a shotgun mic is great for recording sound from a particular person, it can pick up unwanted sound. When there is other noise present, remember that anything inside of the pickup pattern of the mic will also be recorded.

- When using a shotgun mic on a camera, the audio from whomever you are shooting will be recorded along with whatever noise is there behind the person you are shooting. On lower-quality cameras, the mic may also pick up the sound of the camera running (such as tape moving through the camera). This is why it is a good idea to have a boom operator who places the mic above the talent with the mic pointed at the ground. This way the talent's voice will be in the pickup pattern and that pattern then continues straight to the ground. where substantial background noise is less likely.

- Shotgun mics are very susceptible to wind noise. Be sure to attach a blimp or fuzzy to the mic when recording outdoors. These can be purchased from the same store that the microphone comes from.

Cables

The next step in successfully recording good audio is to hook your mics up to your mixer or recording device. To do so you will need the proper cables. Just as a chain is only as strong as its weakest link, your audio recording system is only as good as its cables. Don't. Be sure to buy professional-grade cables (this doesn't necessarily mean the most expensive ones in the fancy packaging) with the proper connectors.

Most audio cables come with one of four types of connectors: mini, phono, RCA, and XLR. The first three are considered unbalanced connections, while the XLR is a balanced connection. You will need a balanced connection if your cable run is going to exceed more than 20 feet.

Field Interviews with a Stick Microphone

A lot of podcasts use the "roving reporter" style of interview where the host holds a "stick" microphone and points it toward the interviewee. This style of podcast is reminiscent of field reporting in broadcast news. So let's take a few pointers from our television friends.

- If your show has a graphic identity, carry it forward by placing your show logo on the microphone. Broadcasters often have microphone flags bearing the logo right on the mic. A quick web search will give you several choices. We usually get ours from www.markertek.com, simply print the logo out onto glossy adhesive, and carefully cut it out with a Xacto knife and mount it. If you're doing a man-on-the-street – show, strongly consider having one. That little piece of plastic has gotten us taken more seriously, more quickly, because people think, "Oh, this is going to be on television."
- Be careful with your microphone position. Common mistakes we see are interviewers shoving a microphone up someone's nose because they've never done an interview before. The proper distance is that from an extended thumb to an extended pinky finger on your hand (around 10 inches).
- Joking aside, it's like you are sharing an ice cream cone. You take a lick. The interviewee takes a lick. Repeat. You can learn how to hold a microphone by watching some broadcast television news.
- Don't lose yourself in the moment. We often see inexperienced interviewers who remember to hold out the microphone for the first time, but then continue to hold it by their own mouth for subsequent questions. It's important that the camera person (or audio person if you have one) is paying attention. Make sure someone on the crew is wearing good headphones and can clearly hear the sound that is being recorded.

Professional XLR audio cables are essential.

Most lower-end camcorders will have unbalanced audio inputs, while more expensive cameras will be equipped with balanced audio connections. Be sure to check out the particular audio connections of the equipment you are using and make sure you have the proper cables and adaptors. We'll explore camera connections in the next chapter.

Mixers and Recording Devices

If you are using multiple microphones on your shoot, you will want to use a field audio mixer to combine your audio sources into one or two channels, which is probably all that your camera is capable of recording (some newer HD cameras can record four channels of audio). A mixer will also boost your audio from mic level, which is a relatively weak audio signal, to line level, which is capable of traveling greater distances.

Most portable field mixers will allow you to combine between two and four audio sources. Many of these mixers have visible VU meters that will allow you to visually monitor the strength of the audio signal and if necessary increase or decrease the signal to optimum recording levels. If you are taping something like a panel discussion with more than four sources of audio, you will need a mixer capable of handling as many as 24 channels. These mixers are not portable (in that you can't carry them on your person), but they can easily be set-up in a location such as a hotel ballroom. While not required, the use of a mixer allows you a lot of control.

In most cases if you are shooting a video podcast you will also be recording your audio on the camera. Most camcorders and prosumer video cameras will allow you to record two channels of audio. Therefore you can use the second channel as a safety. Some people choose to put the shotgun microphone here. Others recommend feeding the mixer's audio, but recording it at a slightly lower volume in case your subjects suddenly talk louder. This will let you avoid microphone clipping at a loud volume.

On-Set Monitoring

 Perhaps the single most important thing you can do while taping a podcast is to be sure someone on your crew is wearing a good set of headphones through which you monitor the sound being recorded by the camera.

Common Errors

Remember it is much easier to add additional sounds to that you have recorded than it is to remove unwanted sound. So if the kid across the street starts to mow his lawn during the middle of your shoot you may want to try greasing his palm with a twenty rather than going with the assumption that you can use a filter to remove this sound during postproduction. Besides making bad assumptions, here are a few more things to look out for.

Mic/Line Level

If you're plugging microphones into a professional camera you are usually presented with a switch labeled "mic/line." If you are running your microphones through a mixer, you generally set it to line level. If the microphones are going directly to the camera, you set it to mic level. What is important here is testing. If you have switches set incorrectly, you will likely get distorted audio that can be unusable. Be sure to check both ends of the cable (that is to say the mixer and the camera).

Dead Batteries

Many microphones and mixers require power sources. A battery is the most likely power source. These might be AA, AAA, or watch battery style. Whichever your microphone or mixer uses, have extra (lots extra). On nearly every shoot we've ever had, the field mixer burns through a battery. Also, the microphones seem to cut out at the least convenient time. If you are using a wireless equipment, you'll go through batteries even faster. A spare package of batteries is much cheaper than delaying your shoot or missing a shot. We keep a compartment just for batteries and make sure it is refilled every time before leaving our shop for a shoot.

Mic Placement

Microphones are great, but only if you use them correctly. Be sure you know the pickup patterns of your microphones, and then position them to capture the speaker. Another common mistake we see is forgetting how people may move on a set. For example, a person doing a technical demonstration may need to look over their right shoulder. If the mic is on the left shoulder, things are going to get pretty quiet. When placing microphones always think about the likely movement of your subject and the pickup capabilities on the mic.

More on Sound?

There are several excellent books and DVDs that focus on sound techniques for video. Here are two we recommend.

Producing Great Sound for Film and Video by Jay Rose
Now Hear This! Superior Sound for Digital Video by Douglas Spotted Eagle and VASST

Crossing Wires

Wise men were right to say, "Don't cross the streams". When microphone cables cross power cables, you can get a lot of electromagnetic hum. Audio cables can be shielded to help minimize this, but it's a good idea to run your audio cables so they do not cross or tangle with other equipment cables. In fact, be sure to tape things down, both for safety and to prevent cables from getting mixed throughout the production.

Our Standard Audio Kit for Podcast Productions

2	Headphones		3	Sennheiser Wireless Mic Gear
1	Sound Devices 2-Channel Mixer		1	Breakaway XLR Mic Cable
1	7-Feet Boom Pole		2	10-Feet XLR Cable
1	Sennheiser Shotgun Microphone with Cover		2	20-Feet XLR Cable
			6	Spare Batteries
1	Shock Mount (connected to pole)		1	Box of Audio Adapters
1	Mathews Grip Head		2	Tram Lavalier Microphone set
1	Boom Pole Mounts		1	M-Audio Digital Recorder

PRO_file_: LetsKnit2gether

LetsKnit2gether is a five- to ten-minute video podcast about knitting produced by Brave New Rocket (www.BraveNewRocket.com). The episodes cover topics like knitting socks, blocking, felting, cables, knitting with ribbon, and lace knitting. LetsKnit2gether (www.LetsKnit2gether.com) focuses on intermediate to advanced techniques and takes special care to show the actual knitting up close with simple and clear instructions. Let'sKnit2gether is frequently featured in the iTunes Store Top 10 podcasts in the Hobbies category.

While many people focus on cameras, Eric Susch recommends keeping an eye on lighting and sound.

"Good audio is the single most important thing. If your viewers can't understand what people are saying they won't care how pretty your pictures are. Good audio is also an unconscious sign of a professional production," says Eric.

"Lighting is the second most important thing. We take a lot of care with the lighting for our demonstration shows. We shoot in our home and have several standard locations in different rooms so there is a bit of variety in the shows. I have very detailed lighting diagrams so that we can set up and break down quickly. We also shoot multiple shows at once so we can save time."

The show also takes "field trips" to knitting events like the Sheep and Wool festivals in New York and Maryland, to capture the spirit of knitting culture. For example, a 2007 field trip took the show to Shea Stadium and a Mets game, for Stitch n Pitch, an event attended by over eight hundred knitters.

CAT Susch, who has been knitting for more than 20 years and develops all the demonstrations, hosts the show. Her husband Eric handles all of the production and editing. Eric leveraged his experience producing shows for the Discovery Channel to create this podcast series. The show is shot entirely in HD, with an emphasis on high production values and enjoyable content.

"We shoot everything in HD and finish to broadcast specifications. We use two different cameras for the two types of shows we do. For the demo shows we shoot with a JVC GY-HD110U," explains Eric. "For our 'field trips' we shoot with a Sony HC1 because it's small and nonthreatening."

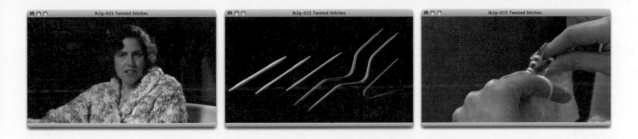

A focus on saving time and money is just one of the lessons learned.

"Shorter is usually better (when in doubt, cut it out!). Podcasting is not time-based like TV, where every show has to be an exact length to fit in a time slot. Don't fall into bad TV habits by adding fluff to fill time because you lack content. Let your content decide how long your show will be. This is one of the advantages of podcasting over TV and your viewers will appreciate the fact that you are treating their time as valuable."

Eric has embraced podcasting. He sees it as a valid alternative to traditional media outlets.

"A few years ago it was becoming clear that broadcast television was changing, and not for the better. Production budgets were getting smaller and smaller. The business is now about volume, with every show getting more and more tabloid to get attention," said Eric Susch. "I started looking for a new outlet. When podcasting began I said to myself, 'How can we get into this and try it without spending any money on it?' Let'sKnit2gether

started basically as a test to see what this new medium can do. CAT had all the knitting expertise (so the 'content' was free) and I had a lot of the equipment and production expertise. We could start a show and give this new medium the ultimate real-world test. Our first year was extremely successful, and our test has become something we want to continue and try to make money with."

Eric is now focusing his professional career on LetsKnit2gether and on developing podcasting and new media programs for others. He is learning a lot as he goes, but offered practical advice to those just starting out.

"Keep it simple. Video podcasting can be whatever you want and that leads to many exciting possibilities. It's impossible to travel down all those roads at the same time, and you can quickly become overwhelmed. Figure out what you want your show to be and stick with it," he says. "Your success is not dependent on one or two episodes—it's based on the show as a whole. That leaves room for a misstep here and there. It's not a big disaster if you have a terrible show. Make any adjustments necessary and continue on."

Gear List

- JVC GY-HD110U camera
- Sony HC1 camera
- Sachtler System tripod
- Sony 17-inch HD LCD Monitor
- Arri Softbank 1 kit that has two 650 fresnels, one 300 fresnel, and a 1K open face with a chimera and an egg crate
- A 30 inch silver/white FlexFill
- Pro Prompter
- Schoeps CMC 5 microphone
- Electrovoice 635AB Wireless Microphone
- BeachTek DXA-2S XLR audio adapterr

5

PRODUCTION: VIDEOGRAPHY

One of the quickest ways to destroy your show's credibility is through bad videography. If your camerawork distracts from the show's content, it can drive an audience away. Many video podcasters do not have formal training in properly using a video camera or composing their shots for artistic impact. We will touch on guiding principles in this chapter to help those less familiar with the craft of videography. Even seasoned pros will find this information useful, because the podcast screen has different rules than a television or theatrical production.

Podcast crews are often lean and multi-talented.

Before we jump into specifics, let's offer an easy-to-remember concept called the KISS methodology. What we mean here is Keep It Simple, Stupid … do not overextend your skills and try to shoot everything with a handheld camera unless you really know how. If you (or your talent) aren't great at doing repeated takes from different angles, simplify and shoot with multiple cameras. The goal with podcast videography is attractive camerawork that can be acquired quickly and consistently. With this in mind, let's start with the first ingredient of great videography, the camera.

Camera Considerations

Choosing the right camera for your podcasts is all about balancing the requirements of the job, the equipment available to you, and your budget. In this chapter, we're not going to attempt to talk you into buying a lot of gear. Rather, we'll focus on different equipment options that have worked well for our productions and share our rationale for using the gear. With that said, you may be in a situation where you don't have a lot of options. With that in mind, we'll also address very affordable "add-ons" that significantly improve production quality or save time.

Let's start by taking a look at essential features that your camera should offer. While you can always get by with less, we find that cameras need a certain level of base performance (after all it's kind of hard to make a car with two flat tires and a missing battery climb a mountain).

Things to Look For

Three CCDs. Cameras utilize charge-coupled devices (CCDs) to capture their images. These are the sensors that convert the image seen by the lens into a signal that can be recorded to tape, disk, or drive. Many consumer-oriented cameras only come with a single CCD, which results in a significantly poorer picture than cameras with three chips. In cameras with three CCDs, a prism is used to split the light entering the lens into red, green, and blue components, and then each component is directed to a single chip solely dedicated to a specific color.

Three CCDs will help capture a better image.

Additionally, you'll see that CCDs are often identified by size. A 2/3-inch CCD is twice as large as a 1/3-inch one and generally will give you better image quality. Three CCDs are an absolute must-have; once you have that squared away you can make decisions based on their quality and your budget.

FireWire Connectivity. Many cameras come with multiple connection types, including USB2 and HDMI. The one that works the best with the most editing applications is FireWire. All Macintosh computers and most PCs include a FireWire port. If they don't

FireWire: A Technology with Many Names

 If you are shopping for FireWire technology, you'll often see it referenced by two additional names. Sony frequently calls the technology i.Link, while others favor the generic IEEE 1394, which refers to the number given to it by the Institute of Electrical and Electronics Engineers. The technology is identical; what is at play here is a resistance to use the FireWire logo and name, which is closely associated with Apple, Inc., which co-developed the technology.

Adding to the confusion is that there is FireWire 400 and FireWire 800. The technology called FireWire 800 uses a 9-pin connection type and is much less common. It is generally used for higher speed hard drives and is usually not found on cameras.

have one, or you need additional ones, adding an expansion card is a simple matter and generally costs less than $75.

When you look at the camera body, you'll generally see one of two types of FireWire connections. The full-size connector is called a 6-pin port. The primary advantage of the 6-pin port is that it is a sturdier connection type. However, many smaller cameras use the 4-pin connection type. While this connector saves space on smaller cameras, it is more prone to damage because it uses a smaller connector type. Be very careful to avoid tension on your FireWire cables, especially if you are using a smaller, 4-port connection type.

Having a FireWire connection will let you load footage from your camera directly into your editing system. This works very well for spot checks, chroma key tests, or sending the client a review clip. You generally do not want to rely on the camera for loading all of your tape, though, as the wear and tear can drastically shorten the life of tape-based cameras. A better option is to purchase an affordable feeder deck such as the Sony DSR-11. Other benefits of FireWire ports include the ability to harness direct to disk recorders and monitoring devices like Adobe's On Location software (which gives you the ability to calibrate your video camera for better results). Quite simply, you can't go wrong with a FireWire port, so make sure your camera has one.

XLR Audio Inputs. While we focused on audio in our last chapter, it's important to look at the bridge between your audio gear and your camera. One audio connection type that is standard in the professional world is XLR. Video cameras use the common 3-pin

XLR cable type, which is also called a balanced audio connector. This works well for professional microphones since they can reduce noise. XLR cables are both twisted and shielded, which helps cut down on interference.

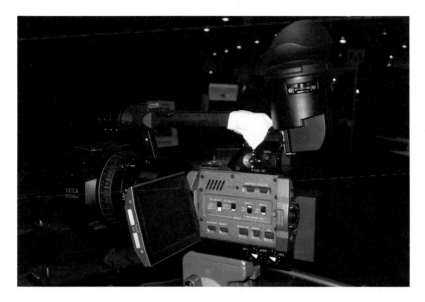

Don't overlook the viewfinder in the eyepiece. This is often just as important as the large flip-out viewfinder. Additionally, you can save battery power by using the smaller viewfinder.

Grayscale/Hi-Resolution Viewfinder. Many users find giant LCD full-color viewfinders to be attractive. The problem is they often hide flaws in your video. Due to the LCD's sharpness and boosted saturation, video may look better than it really is. Try to learn to shoot using both a hi-resolution viewfinder that shows a grayscale image and a reference monitor to check color. If the reference monitor is not an option, then you can use the LCD as a last resort. But you will still want to learn to use the viewfinder to check important details. The benefit of grayscale is that it is often easier to see things like exposure and focus when you remove the distraction of color.

Things to Avoid

Direct to DVD/YouTube/WMV. Many cameras boast features that make your video ready for "instant" distribution. The problem is that the camera is heavily compressing the video. For best results, you want to capture video at as the highest possible quality. You then edit the video together and make any improvements needed. The final step is compression with the intended target in mind. This issue has been addressed in the digital photography world by most professionals by dumping JPEG acquisition in favor of the much more robust camera raw approach.

What Is XLR?

The name XLR connector refers to its original manufacturer, Canon. It was originally called the "Cannon X" series. Canon then released a version that could "click" into place with a latch, called the "Cannon XL." The final variation used a rubber compound to surround the contacts, which gave the abbreviation XLR.

Keep Two Sets of Cables Handy

A mantra that we like to repeat often is this: 90% of all problems are cable problems. A bad cable can destroy your production. From pops in the interview to a flickering client monitor, a bad cable can do all sorts of damage. Cables are cheap, re-shoots are not. To avoid expensive problems keep two sets of audio, video, and FireWire cables with your camera bag. And when a cable goes bad, toss it and replace it.

A simple rule of high-quality web productions is start high, finish low. You should avoid shooting heavily compressed files, because they do not offer you latitude when you are color correcting or compositing, plus they can take significantly longer to process on your computer. As broadband connection speeds continue to increase and server space becomes cheaper and cheaper, sites such as YouTube will inevitably change their specifications to allow larger files to be hosted on their site. By capturing your video in a format that employs less compression you will have the ability to scale your productions to meet changing delivery specifications.

Cell Phone and Digital Photo Cameras. If you are a vlogger (a video blogger) and just want to capture a moment or thought, then you can get by with a camera of this type. But if you want real control with professional audio and video connections, you need to think twice. While many manufactures boast of DVD quality or TV quality, they, quite simply, are lying. Just because a picture is 640 × 480 doesn't mean that it has a proper frame rate and audio quality to match the standards needed by nonlinear editing software. Again, cut corners on your camera and you'll pay for it during the editing stage.

USB Video Conferencing Camera. While it's easy to come by video cameras that are suited for instant messaging and video conferencing, do not be tempted to use these. These cameras generally have poor focus controls as well as inferior lens quality.

Choosing an Acquisition Format

There are several competing tape and acquisition formats on the market. Many formats are tied to specific manufacturers, and you will hear competing claims of superiority as rival companies try to establish dominance. That's not to say that formats don't matter—they do in many cases. But let's start with the bigger question: Should you shoot standard- or high-definition video?

Standard-Definition Video

There are many compelling reasons to shoot your video podcasts in standard definition (SD), the first being financial. SD video equipment is well established and readily available. As such, it costs less to use an SD workflow. Cameras cost less, tape and storage media cost less, capture devices cost less, and so on. Because podcasting is generally a price-sensitive marketplace, standard definition is a logical choice.

When using multiple cameras, try to match manufacturers and models.

Plus if you're looking to create video podcasts, nearly all of the shows on the market are delivered at 640 × 480 or 320 × 240. Both of these sizes can be easily generated by an SD video camera with minimal processing. It is important to note that SD just refers to a category and not a particular format. You will encounter several video formats that are all considered SD.

DV/DVCPRO/DVCAM. The digital-video (DV) format launched in 1994 was originally intended for use by prosumers and consumers. Many pros embraced it, however, because of its ease of use and price competitiveness. The format is very space efficient—it

only requires 12 GB of storage for an hour of footage. It is also very easy to load as these cameras and decks use the FireWire protocol. It also supports both 4:3 and 16:9 aspect ratios, thus extending videography options.

There have been some notable variants on the DV standard. Sony released the DVCAM format, which moves the tape 50% faster through the camera (resulting in fewer dropouts). Panasonic also developed the DVCPRO formats targeted at professional use. The tapes for DVCPRO are much thicker and sturdier, which works well for traditional tape-based editing.

The DV format works very well for podcasting and is widely embraced by video podcasters due to its balance of cost and quality. The one area where DV footage is particularly problematic, though, is chroma keying. If you are looking to use blue or green screen technology with virtual sets, you should stay away from DV because it does not key well. Otherwise, DV should be your strongest contender for podcast productions.

DVCPRO 50. The DVCPRO 50 format is an extension of DV technology and is available in many of Panasonic cameras. The DVCPRO 50 format uses dual encoders to double the bit rate of data being recorded. This format uses the same tapes as the DVCPRO format but consumes tape twice as fast when recording. In addition to doubling the data being recorded, the format also uses a higher chroma subsampling, which produces better color fidelity and image quality. As such, DVCPRO 50 is much better suited for chroma keying. DVCPRO 50 also supports shooting both 4:3 and 16:9, which adds more flexibility to your productions.

Betacam SP/DigiBeta/Betacam SX. While a venerable format with a rich history, Sony's Betacam formats don't see much action in the podcasting space. Many established video production companies utilize beta gear (which is a high-quality format). The significantly higher cost of the equipment, though, can quickly balloon a podcast's budget. As such, you should be wary of working with footage acquired on Betacam. Additionally, the technology is often considered "dead" by media pros because it is waning in popularity as digital (and more affordable) options become new standards. Sony has practically abandoned the format in that they are not developing new products to sell and only carry one or two models of decks for each format.

XDCAM. A much more viable format for those podcasters who prefer to work with Sony gear is the XDCAM format. XDCAM is an optical, disc-based system introduced in 2003. It acquires directly to affordable discs that often sell for less than $30. Each disc can hold between 45 minutes and 2 hours of content, depending on the acquisition approach taken with the camera. Due to the affordable media recording options and the relative ease of loading footage, XDCAM cameras are proving popular with the podcasting crowd.

High-Definition Video

High-definition (HD) video is more expensive to work with. It requires more robust hard drives, better monitors, more expensive cameras, greater skill, and the list goes on. Acquiring video at High Definition may seem contradictory when the goal is to deliver small, web-ready files at an affordable cost. With that said, many podcasters do just that. The decision to shoot HD video is really about future-proofing your footage. Reasons to shoot a podcast in HD include

- The footage has residual value and will be used in future productions.
- The podcast is going to be distributed in multiple sizes and formats, including devices like Apple TV and TiVo HD digital video recorders.
- The project has additional distribution channels like broadcast and HD-DVD or Blu-ray.
- You offer a premium subscription service with paid downloads for HD files.
- You have easy access to HD equipment and want to rack up additional experience with HD projects.

It is essential to stress that working in HD adds cost to a project. We find that HD projects tend to cost 30% to 50% more to complete than SD projects. This is due in part to the aforementioned

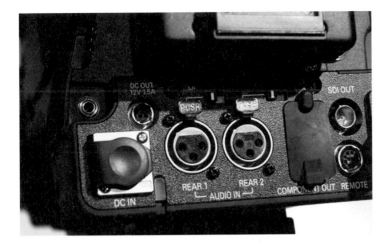

costs associated with gear. Additionally, you will spend more time on tasks like rendering for graphics and effects as well as see longer compression times when finishing the project. We are not saying you should avoid HD—the many affordable cameras and options on the market are very desirable—just be aware of the additional costs involved. There are many HD formats on the market; here are the three most commonly used by podcasters.

High-Definition Standard Sizes and Frame Rates

When it comes to HD, there are a lot of "flavors." Broadcasters have established the following standard HD formats

Type	Dimensions	Frames per second	Scanning method
720 24 p	1280 × 720 pixels	23.976	Progressive
720 25 p	1280 × 720 pixels	25	Progressive
720 30 p	1280 × 720 pixels	29.97	Progressive
720 50 p	1280 × 720 pixels	50	Progressive
720 60 p	1280 × 720 pixels	59.94	Progressive
1080 24 p	1920 × 1080 pixels	23.976	Progressive
1080 25 p	1920 × 1080 pixels	25	Progressive
1080 30 p	1920 × 1080 pixels	29.97	Progressive
1080 60 p	1920 × 1080 pixels	59.94	Progressive
1080 50 i	1920 × 1080 pixels	25 (50 fields per second)	Interlaced
1080 60 i	1920 × 1080 pixels	29.97 (59.94 fields per second)	Interlaced

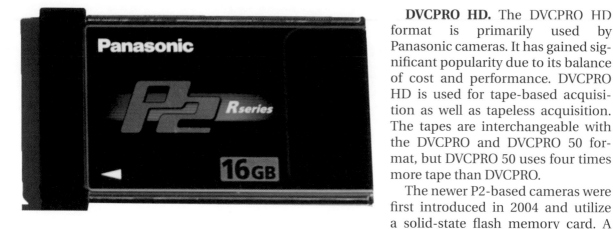

DVCPRO HD. The DVCPRO HD format is primarily used by Panasonic cameras. It has gained significant popularity due to its balance of cost and performance. DVCPRO HD is used for tape-based acquisition as well as tapeless acquisition. The tapes are interchangeable with the DVCPRO and DVCPRO 50 format, but DVCPRO 50 uses four times more tape than DVCPRO.

The newer P2-based cameras were first introduced in 2004 and utilize a solid-state flash memory card. A P2 card can record either DVCPRO 50 or HD footage. The P2 postproduction workflow takes a little time to master, but using P2 cards works well for many podcasters because you can plug them directly into a computer, transfer the files, and start editing. While the cards are expensive, they can be reused nearly infinitely. This saves money on tape stock and eliminates the need for an expensive deck.

HDV/ProHD. The HDV format is a very popular format for entry-level HD. This inexpensive format compresses HD video using MPEGH-2 compression (the same as DVDs) and then records it to tapes identical to the mini-DV format. This compression can create some workflow issues during postproduction and often requires extra steps. Nevertheless, since it is the least expensive way to move into HD production, many podcasters and video professionals have adopted it.

More on HDV

Looking to find out more on HDV? A useful book is *HDV: What You NEED to Know!* by Douglas Spotted Eagle. This book offers useful advice and essential information on HDV workflows. Find out more at www.VASST.com.

HDV was originally developed by JVC and Sony, which were later joined by Canon and Sharp. These companies manufacture several different models of cameras targeted at both consumers and prosumers. The format has also been extended by JVC and called ProHD. The main difference is that it can natively shoot 720p at 24 frames per second.

XDCAM HD. Sony's XDCAM format was discussed earlier in the chapter. Sony has extended it to offer an HD option. It is important to note that not all XDCAM cameras can shoot HD, so check your options when renting or buying a camera. Sony's XDCAM HD options offer different bit rates, so be sure to strike the right balance of file size and quality. You'll want to use the higher bit rates for more visually complex materials like fast-moving shots, scenics, and large crowds.

Interviewer Tips

Becoming a good interviewer is an acquired skill that takes training and practice. For the less experienced, here are a few helpful pointers.

- Edit in the camera. Encourage short answers and come back to topics again. Better to focus on good, tight answers than trying to cobble together six takes to make your point.
- Avoid enumeration or the phrase "Like I said before." It is highly likely that you will use only part of the answer (such as step three, without steps one and two).
- Ask leading, open-ended questions … being sure to ask a single question only.
- Don't be afraid to stop and start over. Do not let an answer ramble on. Smiles and nods can let subjects know they have make their point and can stop talking.

Camera Support Options

Many podcasters shoot their video without using a tripod. This is a terrible mistake as very few people should actually shoot their video handheld. While handheld video can be used stylistically to great effect, it is rarely useful when it comes to video that is intended for the web. The slight (or not-so-slight) movement of the camera can result in pixelization or softening when the video is compressed for podcast.

Now some of you think you're better than this … let's take a simple test. Stand up and extend your arm out directly in front of you with your palm raised (like you are a traffic cop stopping traffic). Now hold that position for 60 seconds without moving. Look at your hand … is it twitching at all? Chances are … yes. It's not your fault—you're overworked, overcaffeinated, and suffer from a lack of rest (in other words, you are part of the modern workforce). Shooting smooth, handheld video is very difficult. Here are a few options for camera support that you can consider.

Tripod. It should go without saying, but use a tripod. There are several price points out there on tripods, depending on how tall you want the tripod to rise. The head of the tripod is also critical, as you'll likely need it to smoothly pan and tilt for your productions. A top-of-the-line fluid head can cost thousands of dollars by itself. Luckily, with the advent of DV prosumer cameras there has been an influx of tripods with decent fluid heads at reachable price points. Pros use tripods all the time; they are a given. Simply put, use a tripod!

Steadicam. The name Steadicam is often applied to several models of camera stabilizers. In fact, Steadicam is a brand name for a type of unit originally developed by cinematographer Garret Brown in 1972. The units are meant to help capture smooth video when walking or jogging with a camera. The operator generally wears a special vest, which has a metal support arm that is stabilized by a spring and counter balance system. Through the years, many different variations have been created. You can find out much more by visiting www.steadicam.com and looking at the different models. For podcasters, the Steadicam Merlin offers a great number of features at an affordable price.

Other Options. There are many other camera support options on the market for almost any budget point. Here are a few worth looking at that can help stabilize your camera and give you better-looking video when not using a tripod:

- **Frezzi Stable-Cam** (www.frezzi.com)
- **Fig Rig** (www.services.manfrotto.com/figrig)
- **Turtle X** (www.easyrig.com)

Tapeless Acquisition

Earlier we discussed Panasonic's P2 and Sony's XDCAM formats. Both offer acquisition of video material without using tape. These are not the only solutions; there are hard drive units that can work with almost any camera that offers a FireWire port. But why forego tape and shoot directly to a magnetic or solid-state media? There are several potential reasons.

Be sure to spot check your tapeless recorder to make sure it is indeed recording.

Benefits of Tapeless Acquisition

There are many benefits of tapeless acquisition that can impact a podcaster. The biggest is the speed at which you can move from shooting to editing. Eliminating the need to log and capture tape can save you a significant amount of time. You can begin editing your material as fast as you can transfer the media to an editing system (which is often 10–15 times faster than loading a tape).

Other benefits include that the tapeless media can be used again and again. While media like P2 may seem expensive at first, value is achieved over time because you do not need to keep buying tape stock. You can also play back your footage quickly and review your shots right in the field, deciding to drop bad takes before ever going into an edit session.

Tapeless media can also make it easier to share your footage with others. We often make multiple copies of media so that several individuals can begin editing at once. We also find it simple to turn interview clips into MP3 files if we need to get material transcribed quickly (the process of turning interviews into a text log). This can be helpful if the material needs input from project participants who'd rather look at a paper log or searchable text file.

Don't Edit Directly from Tapeless Media

While you often can edit directly from a tapeless acquisition drive or disk, it's generally a good idea to transfer the media first to an editing hard drive. This will reduce wear and tear on the equipment and make it last longer.

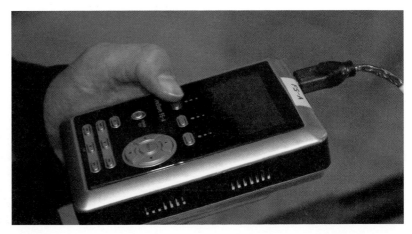

Drawbacks of Tapeless Acquisition

For every benefit, there is of course a drawback. Most notably, tapeless acquisition is new, and as such it can cost more initially to get started. We have always waited until we experience growing pains before investing in new equipment. Before you rush out and plunk down a bunch of money, evaluate how much time (hence dollars) you are spending by loading tape into your computer. If you are producing one 10-minute podcast a week, tapeless acquisition is likely overkill.

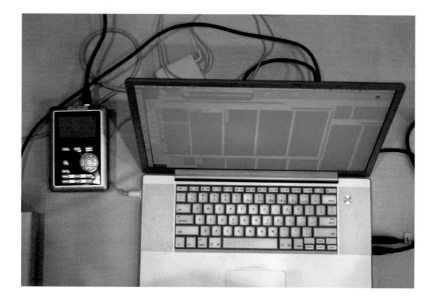

Another drawback can be that tapeless acquisition can create the need for an additional person on set, often called the data assistant. This person fills a role similar to the person on film shoots who is in charge of reloading and handling the film needed by the cameras. We cannot emphasize enough the need to have that individual on the set if you're working with P2 or hard drive–based media. On our shoots, we generally make two backup copies of each card or disk. The first copy is loaded into the nonlinear editing system via an import command, which places the media on an editing hard drive. The second copy is a disk image, which we back up to a temporary hard drive. After the shoot, we burn Blu-ray discs for our archives and make a copy if the client wants a set of "master tapes."

Which brings up the next point. Without tape, you may have no backup. Be sure your tapeless media is redundant. You'll need to make a mirrored copy of your drive to keep your media ready to use. You'll also need to explore cheaper archive solutions like a

DLT drive or Blu-ray DVDs to create affordable archives that can be stored for long-term backup.

Tapeless Acquisition Technology

If you've decided to explore tapeless acquisition, let us offer a few solutions. By now, you have heard us discuss Panasonic's P2 and Sony's XDCAM at length. While both of these are great solutions, they are more expensive than the FireWire crowd may want to spend.

The most popular solution for both DV and HDV cameras is the direct-to-edit hard drive unit manufactured by companies like Focus Enhancements (www.focusinfo.com). Essentially, these units are battery-operated hard drives that can take a video signal out of your camera and create clips on the fly, then store them on a hard drive. Every time you press the start/stop button on your camera, a new clip is created. Additionally, the clips have a time code identical to what is being recorded on tape. This makes a great backup because you can always reload from tape if your hard drive fails and your media goes offline.

The basic recorders are priced around $800 for 3 hours of storage; larger capacities are available, including units that let you record for an entire production day. When you are finished recording, you plug the unit into a computer and transfer the media to an editing system. We have found that these units save a ton of time and, for a relatively active production company, pay for themselves in a few jobs.

On-Camera Considerations

Here are a few extra tips to help less-experienced on-camera talent or interviewees. You can modify this list or e-mail it as-is to the talent ahead of time.

- Bring at least one alternative set of clothing.
- Herringbone, stripes, or small patterns do not look good on camera. Avoid vivid patterns, plaids, and geometric shapes.
- Please keep your jewelry simple.
- Do not wear bright white. Cream, eggshell, or light gray are preferrable.
- Unless told otherwise, maintain eye contact with your interviewer throughout the interview.
- Relax.

Shooting for Portability

When you are shooting video for a podcast, you need to remember that the podcast screen behaves differently than a movie or television screen. While podcasts can be delivered to television sets with relative ease, most users are watching podcasts in either of two places, a computer monitor or a portable media player. These devices have a few things in common.

The Screen is Small. We tended to favor tighter shots; that is a conscious decision. Remember, video will likely be seen at a small size (some players are as small as 2 inches diagonally. Therefore, there are a few things you need to keep in mind when composing your shots. Tight shots work better than wide shots since much of the detail will be lost by the time your footage reaches the small screen.

Action Safe Is the New Title Safe. Traditionally, videographers have learned to frame their shots to protect both the action-safe and title-safe areas of the frame. In the world of TV broadcasting, monitors do not necessarily display the entire frame of video. For this reason, there are two cropped zones within the frame; both are equidistance on all sides from the edges of the full frame. The larger of the two zones is referred to as *action safe* and the slightly smaller zone is called *title safe*.

The thinking is that when shooting or editing if you keep the action inside the action-safe zone and any key information such as graphics and text inside the title-safe zone, then it will display properly on even the most restrictive of monitors. In the world of podcasting, you'll see the entire video clip. Because of this, we have basically done away with the concept of title safe and now just keep what we really want on viewers' screens inside of action safe. This allows a little bit of padding (like a margin) but maximizes the smaller screen.

Avoid Shaky Video. Because your source video is going to get highly compressed before it is delivered as a podcast, it is important that your shots be as steady as possible. Podcast compression saves space by repeating pixels that don't change from frame to frame. As such, your video will be *much* clearer if it is a stable shot. Remember, shaky video doesn't compress well and results in muddy looking video.

Packing Lists for a Two-Camera DV Package

2	Panasonic DVX-100 camera
6	5400mah batteries
2	Battery charger with AC adaptor
2	Sharpie markers

20	Mini-DV tape stock
1	Video adaptors and barrels bag
1	Leatherman multitool
1	Lens cloth

Don't forget your AC adapters to save battery power.

1	JVC 10-inch field monitor (two input)
1	Slate and dry-erase markers
2	25-foot BNC cable
1	Anti-shine powder w/ applicators
1	Makeup kit

2	Focus enhancement: FS-4 (Firestore) with cables, batteries, charger
1	Cartoni tripod with plate
1	Sachtler tripod with plate

Recognize Lower Frame Rates. Web video and even podcasts can have reduced frame rates. Combine this with lower data rates and you want to avoid much camera motion. Lots of pans or zooms tend to break down during compression process. For this reason, we recommend favoring straight cuts rather than creating in-camera effects.

Evaluate Using 16 × 9. Shooting video in 16 × 9 aspect ratio has become quite popular. However, most podcasts are delivered in the 4 × 3 aspect ratio. If you decide to shoot in the 16 × 9 format, you should protect your shots for center cut during post-production. This concept is similar to the action-safe/title-safe concept described earlier, but in this case only a portion of the side of each frame will be trimmed during the edit.

PRO*file*: The Canyons

The Canyons is a ski resort in Park City Utah (www.thecanyons.com). To promote the resort and its activities, the owners started producing video podcasts in late 2005. The idea came from videographer/photographer Dan Campbell.[1]

"I am always trying to keep up with the new technologies. When I first started seeing the voice-only podcasts, I thought it was a great way to bring your media to a wide audience," said Campbell. "I downloaded the very first voice podcast from www.photoshopusertv.com as I was learning Photoshop CS2. They went to video soon after that. I knew right then that this was cool and would soon become very popular. So I invented the job for myself and took my proposal to The Canyons."

[1] Dan Campbell can be reached at +1-435-513-1088 or freewill79@hotmail.com.

This go-getter attitude is common amongst podcasters, who often have to provide the spark for innovation. Campbell says that the podcast series he produces for The Canyons resort has been well received.

"This podcast is for our guests to view from wherever they may be. It's really just a great way to show some of the activities, places, and personalities we have at The Canyons," said Campbell. "I do a weekly podcast that covers anything from heading out at 4:30 a.m. with the ski patrol for avalanche work to our annual pond-skimming competition."

To capture this dynamic content, Campbell uses some specialized gear. He relies on both video and still cameras to capture the action. He also utilizes HD to get the best image possible. To reach the action, Campbell uses a Cablecam and dolly system; these get the camera above the action and open up many creative options.

The podcasts Campbell has produced have helped him land additional work. He spends time working with Matchstick Productions on their Emmy-award-winning TV series for Rush HD called "*FOCOSED*." He has also landed a new podcast series on racing.

"I am off to the Baja 1000 (this year) to do podcasts," Campbell says. "These podcasts will be edited from the back of a moving support vehicle and uploaded via satellite. The producers have paid for much of my equipment and kept me up with the latest and greatest technology."

While Campbell likes to work with top equipment, he does recognize that equipment should not be a barrier to those who want to start podcasting.

"Podcasts can be really easy to make, especially video podcasts. You don't need expensive equipment and new computers," explains Campbell. "Have fun with it and just start with anything. Don't be embarrassed about your first few shows—they will get better with time. You will always find an audience for whatever you decide to do."

"If you are filming handheld shots, keep your elbows close to your chest and hold that camera still, or put it on a tripod. Frame your subject so that if you were watching them on a TV they would be looking across the screen not out the side. Also, be sure to keep your horizon line straight."

He said that podcasters should look to improve their post-production as well.

"Learn the basics of your editing software," Campbell advises. "Learn a few things that will set you apart from the rest, like de-interlacing. If you are doing just simple podcast and are just learning how to edit, use an easy product like iMovie and just keep it simple. Don't try to make your video all cool with effects and fades. They just take up bandwidth and will make your video too big to upload to the web."

Gear List

- Panasonic AG-HVX200 HD camera
- Sony HDR-HC3 HDV Handycam with waterproof housing and helmet mount
- Sony DCR-VX 1000 (NTSC)
- Sony DSR-PD100 Camcorder (PAL)
- Canon 40D
- Canon 20D
- Canon EF 70–200 mm f/2.8 L IS USM Lens
- 10–22 mm, 28–105 and two speedlight 580ex flashes
- 5–25 ft dolly system, 250 ft Cablecam
- Photoflex White/Gold LiteDisc

Campbell does recommend learning to make the most from the gear you do have. This takes both practice and training.

ACQUIRING ADDITIONAL SOURCES

The whole point of creating a video podcast is to use the power of images to educate, entertain, or motivate your audience. Without compelling visuals, you have just a bunch of talking heads. Depending on your style of podcast, you may need photos, videos, slides, screen captures, or motion graphics. Additionally, a music identity can be helpful to give your show more life. In this chapter we'll explore the many options for footage and audio that you can use to tell a story. Professional podcasts need the "whole package" to complete the viewing experience.

Video podcasts take more than just camera footage. Flexible tools like Apple Motion can be used to create show titles quickly.

Working with B Roll

The term *B Roll* harkens back to film days. It would often be necessary to splice together two interview clips, which would be on the A-roll film. By using additional footage from the *B Roll*, the jump could be covered. The term has since evolved to be more encompassing and now generally refers to videos that are used to help enhance or tell the story besides the on-camera interviews. There are several sources for *B Roll*, but you need to start thinking about it early on with your productions.

1. **Archive Materials.** There are several sources of publicly available footage that can be freely used in video projects. This material generally comes from government-funded archives (such as the United States National Archives). There may be small fees involved to get copies of footage, but the material can be often used with few or no restrictions. A great place to start your search is www.archives.gov/research/formats/film-sound-video.html. Another place you can browse is www.archive.org, where you'll find several different collections (just be sure to read the usage rights for the footage you want to use).

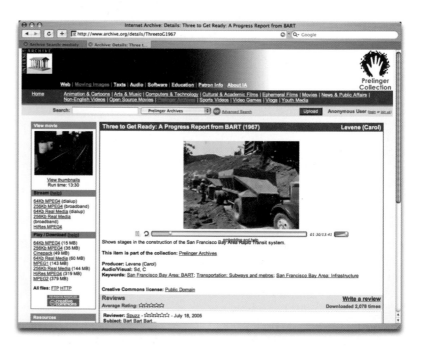

Several hi-resolution clips from the Prelinger collection are available at www.archives.org.

2. **Trade and Business Groups.** You can find professional groups on almost any topic or industry. These groups often have footage or photos that they will share (don't just take it from their website; contact their communications or

media relations departments). Additionally, groups such as chambers of commerce and tourism often have great footage that they can make available to you.

3. **Old Productions.** If we are producing web video for a client, we'll often ask for copies of previous videos they have made. This can be a great source for video in a podcast. Your own archive is also a great place to start if you have rights to the images.

4. **Plan Ahead.** You'll may have great things happening on your set or nearby. You should leave time in the schedule to go and acquire footage. We often bring an extra camera on location so the producer can step away and capture some more footage. This all ties back to the advice of having a multi-talented crew. You'll often be able to cut a person free from your set to gather visuals. What's important is that you generate a checklist prior to the shoot day. List your anticipated needs and then quickly move to capture the material.

Bringing a second camera on your shoots (ideally an identical model) will allow you to capture additional footage.

5. **Stock Footage.** If you can't procure, acquire, or locate footage, you can often buy it. Stock footage costs can vary greatly; the two biggest factors in cost are uniqueness of footage and exclusivity of use. There are several vendors for stock footage. Here are a few that we turn to
   - **Artbeats** (www.artbeats.com)
   - **CNN ImageSource** (www.imagesource.cnn.com)
   - **Digital Juice—Video Traxx** (www.digitaljuice.com)
   - **iStockPhoto** (www.istockphoto.com/video.php)
   - **Revostock** (www.revostock.com)
   - **Rocketclips** (www.rocketclips.com)
   - **Shutterstock Footage** (www.footage.shutterstock.com)

Stock Footage Is Not Custom Footage

A few years ago we were making a web promo video for a corporate client that was holding a meeting in Las Vegas. Our client was firmly convinced that a stock footage shot existed of an Elvis impersonator climbing into a Pink '57 Cadillac and waving to the camera (it doesn't).

The client was also convinced they could take a camera into a casino and videotape gambling (you can't). But we were able to find stock footage of gambling that was shot with actors on a movie set (which looked great and was affordable). We also used stock photography to extend our visual count without taxing our budget. Finally, we got great shots from the Las Vegas tourism board at no cost.

With a little planning and creative thought, your story can be richly illustrated. If you happen to know where we could find that Elvis shot though, let us know. We'd like to make that client happy.

Working with Photos

Many podcast producers overlook the power of still photography. In our experience, photos are a fantastic alternative to video. Photos are generally easier to find or acquire, and thus less expensive and more plentiful. Adding gentle movement to a photo can create a video-like. But mixing photos and video takes a little bit of work. Here are the key points.

1. **Finding Images.** Besides taking your own photos, you'll often need to do some research. The Internet is filled with thousands of sources for stock photos; a simple web search will inundate you with hits. Rather than sending you on a hunt and peck mission, let us offer two great resources. The Raster|Vector weblog covers computer graphics, and it offers a list of government websites with images available for free use. You can find the directory at www.rastervector.com/resources/free/free.html. If you are looking for generous folks willing to share their photos, then check out Creative Commons (www.creativecommons.org). Just be sure to check the requirements for an image's use.

2. **Enhancing Images.** We've never come across a direct-from-camera photo that couldn't be improved. Some of the most common adjustments to photos intended for podcast screens are boosting the saturation and adjusting the gamma or levels for the image. The number one software application for these tasks is Adobe Photoshop. If you need to prep images for use in video, be sure to check out the website: www.PhotoshopforVideo.com. There you'll find a bunch of articles and a podcast on preparing still images for use with digital video.

Google Image Search Is Not a Candy Store

Just because an image is free to view on the Internet does not mean it can be used freely. We know many producers who turn to web search tools like Google Image Search to find photos for their videos. This is generally illegal and can get you into a lot of trouble. There are many affordable stock photo websites as well as photo communities where images are freely shared. Don't be lazy; it might get you sued.

3. **Sizing Images.** For maximum image clarity, it's a good idea to properly size your images to match your editing screen size. Otherwise your editing software will have to scale the images. This leads to an increase in render times and a major drop in image sharpness. While there are several ways of doing this, one of the easiest is to use Adobe Photoshop. For a detailed tutorial on how to size your images, see the book's companion website.

4. **Avoiding JPEGs.** While not exactly malevolent, JPEGs should at least be considered evil. After all, the file type loses additional quality with each File save. The compression scheme used in JPEG files is also problematic when mixed with many common video formats. This can lead to jittery images and flashes. Remember that JPEGs are a web distribution format … the only reason some digital cameras use JPEGs is that they are targeting consumers or trying to reduce the cost of storage media. You should either shoot your images as Camera RAW files or batch convert your JPEG files to an uncompressed format like TIFF or PICT. Trust us when we say, avoid JPEGs.

5. **Motion Control.** One additional technique when working with stills is employing motion control to animate your photos. Some users call this the Ken Burns effect. By animating a photo, you can create zooms and pans to help guide the viewer's eyes through a photo. This technique has been popularized by many documentary filmmakers and is quite effective.
   - For a free web tutorial, visit Creative Cow's website. (www.library.creativecow.net/articles/harrington_richard/doc_style.php)
   - For a full-length DVD, you can try our Motion Control title. (www.vasst.com)

Working with Screen Captures

If you are producing technical training or need to show something like a website or a video game, then you'll need to use a screen capture tool. There are software programs that allow you to record what is happening on your computer's screen. The software can create a video file and store it on a hard drive so you can edit it with your nonlinear editing software.

Screen capture software is needed if you want to record a computer screen for creating how-to tutorials or demonstrations.

We have found that getting high-quality screenshots can be quite tricky. Fortunately, we've had lots of practice in working with these tools. There are several factors that contribute to success; here are the key things we've learned.

1. **Give Your System a Boost.** In order to use screen capture tools, you'll need a pretty powerful computer. Be sure to boost your system's RAM memory; screen capture software needs plenty of it. You'll also want at least a 128 MB graphics card so you can drive two sources. A dedicated-capture hard drive connected via FireWire or SATA is also needed.

Screen Capture Software

While there are several choices out there, here are a few proven ones that do a great job.

- **iShowU** (www.shinywhitebox.com). This tool creates remarkable computer screens for Mac users. It is reasonably priced and does a great job of writing files to disk.
- **Snapz Pro** (www.AmbrosiaSW.com). This is another Mac-only tool for capturing both static and motion screens. This tool is very established, with many users.
- **Camtasia Studio** (www.techsmith.com). This is a PC-only solution that writes very small files. It can then write out to virtually any video format.

2. **Try to Capture at the Size You Need.** If you'd like to get the best results, capture at the size you need. For example, use the square pixel equivalent of 640 × 480 if you are editing a 4:3 podcast. It's important to note that you may need to use a higher resolution monitor setting, such as 800 × 600 or 1024 × 768. If this is the case, you can compress the files after capture and resize to a non-square pixel size like 720 × 480.

3. **Or Just Capture Larger Than You Need.** If you'd like to have more flexibility during the edit, you can capture the video larger than you need. Then simply bring the video

iShowU can capture full-screen video at standard frame rates, including 24p.

into a resolution-independent nonlinear editor (such as Premiere Pro or Final Cut Pro). These types of nonlinear editing packages allow you to load images that are bigger than standard video sizes. Once you've edited the screen capture in your timeline, you can apply scale and position values to adjust what the viewer sees.

4. **Capture at the Right Frame Rate.** One area that can be problematic with screen capture is frame rate. Some software tools support capturing at video native frame rates. However, you really need a powerful computer to perform these styles of capture. If you can't get a consistent frame rate, we recommend running your captured files through a compression tool and converting to a consistent frame rate. Ideally your file will end up at 29.97 or 25 fps to match NTSC and PAL, respectively, or the newer 23.98 which is used by most 24p cameras.

5. **Choose a Proper Codec.** If you need to capture a computer screen you'll need to avoid the DV codec. A codec is a video format's compressor/decompressor. For best results, you'll want to minimize the compression applied to the screen capture. Be sure to check which "uncompressed" formats your nonlinear edit system supports.

Working with Speaker Support/Slides

Many speakers utilize slides to reinforce key points. Common software tools include Microsoft PowerPoint and Apple Keynote. These tools can be used to create text and informational graphics that can be quite effective. While these programs can create effective visuals, you'll need to process the images a bit to make them ready for podcasting.

1. **Design Slides Properly.** By default, most slides are not optimized for video. Don't worry. It's a pretty easy fix; just follow these rules.
   - Don't go too close to the outermost edge. Leave at least a 10% margin around the outside edge.
   - Increase the size of your type. The podcast screen is pretty small; use a larger and thicker font.
   - Simplify your message. Try reducing the length of your bullet points and spreading your slides' content across multiple slides.
   - Increase contrast of text to background. For best results try using light text over a dark background.

Analog Screen Captures

Sometimes, capturing a computer screen using a software tool will be impossible. For example, you may need to record the screens of multiple presenters at a conference or you may have to capture a video source directly from a projector. Don't worry, this too is possible if you use an analog video capture device. The biggest drawback is that the files will likely be larger and a little less clear than the software capture tools.

In order to successfully capture a computer screen's analog signal, you'll need the following.

- A computer that is capable of mirroring its video output so you can see what you are doing on the computer's monitor and still drive an image on a plugged-in device such as a projector or a second monitor.

- A scan converter that lets you feed in the computer's image via a VGA or DVI connection and then converts the signal into analog video. These devices are readily available if you are looking for an S-Video connection type. For maximum image quality however, you should look for a scan converter that offers a component connection such as those from Comprehensive/Kramer.

- A video capture device that accepts analog inputs. Ideally this device will allow resolutions above DV compression. You may already have a device like a capture card or breakout box that allows you to capture directly into your computer. Slightly less desirable, you could record to a high-quality tape format and then capture.

- High-speed hard drives that can work with the uncompressed video. It's important to note that the files can be quite large and demanding if you are used to a DV workflow.

- Editing software that supports an uncompressed workflow. You will want to have very high quality sequence settings so the screens are as easy to see as possible.

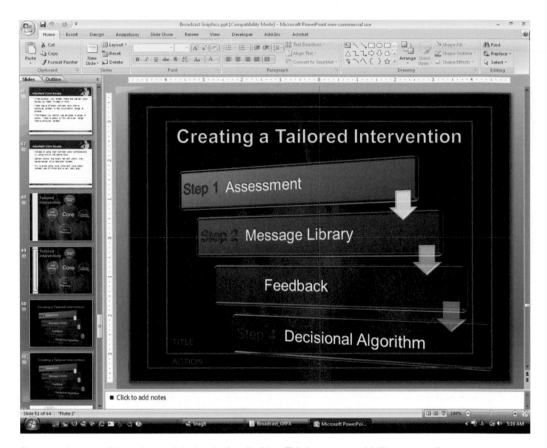

Be sure to leave a slight pad around the border for all slides. This improves readability on a smaller screen.

2. **Export from PowerPoint.** Microsoft PowerPoint makes it easy to save your slides as graphic files. PowerPoint supports seven different graphic formats, including the versatile TIFF and PNG formats.
   - To save your slideshow as a series of still graphics, open your presentation in Microsoft PowerPoint 2007.
   - Click the Office button and choose Save As > Other Formats. Near the bottom of the Save dialog box is a Save as type: drop-down menu. Pick the file format you need (such as TIFF).
   - Specify a location for the files on your hard drive and click Save.
   - PowerPoint then gives you three options: export Every Slide, Current Slide Only, or Cancel.
3. **Export from Keynote.** If you are using a Mac, you should strongly consider using Apple's Keynote application, which is part of iWork. This program is similar to PowerPoint (and can even open PowerPoint files). There are two key

Apple Keynote offers several export options, including graphic and movie files.

differences that make Keynote desirable for preparing slides for a podcast.

- Keynote anti-aliases the text on the slide. This process helps reduce flickering text and makes it look better on a video screen.
- Keynote can export slide animations (such as charts) in a QuickTime format. This adds a lot of life to your podcast.

4. **Process Your Images with Photoshop.** If you've exported your slides as still images, you'll need to do a little work to optimize the images for the screen. This is because most slides are built at a larger size than video (1024 × 768 as opposed to 720 × 480). Using Adobe Photoshop (CS2 or later) you can quickly fix each image by using the Actions palette. You'll find a set of actions called Video Actions by clicking the submenu and loading them.

- Use the DVD Slideshow actions to reformat the slides to fit a standard video screen. This will scale the slides and convert them to non-square pixels so they work in a video timeline.
- Run the Interlace Flicker Removal action to reduce text shimmering.
- You can use the command File > Automate > Batch to run an action on an entire folder of images. This saves time and fixes all of your slides at once.

To load Photoshop's Video Actions, click the triangle in the upper right-hand corner.

Motion Graphics

If you want your podcast to stand out from the clutter, motion graphics are the way to succeed. By giving your show a polished graphical identity, you make it easier for your audience to connect with your program. A well-designed graphics package can help establish the topic of your show as well as reinforce its personality and style. The show's graphics essentially create its brand. This is essential to both attracting and maintaining your audience.

Technology of Choice

Several tools for creating graphics are available to podcasters. Which tools you use will be a matter of availability and skill level. When it comes to motion graphics, you should see the software as being part of a bigger toolkit. As such, it is common to use several tools on a project. The four most common graphic tools are:

- **Adobe Photoshop.** The one graphics tool that is almost universal is Adobe Photoshop. If you understand Photoshop, most other graphics tools will make sense. Photoshop integrates well with nearly every motion graphics and video-editing tool on the market. Before you invest time learning another tool, start with Photoshop. It's important to focus on graphics that look good when they're not moving; then these can be animated. You will learn to use technology for compositing and design. Plus, compared to other graphics software, Photoshop is easier to learn. This is due in large part to the vast number of books, websites, and even podcasts about the program.

- **Adobe After Effects.** After Effects is often called "Photoshop with a timeline." It has very close integration with Photoshop, in that it can easily import layered Photoshop files, which can be animated. Adobe After Effects is a wonderful, yet very complex tool that will take an investment of time to learn. However, the investment pays off in that After Effects knowledge is a very marketable skill.

- **Apple Motion.** If your workflow is primarily Apple-based, then you should strongly consider integrating Apple Motion into your toolset. While Motion can work with keyframes much like After Effects does, it has additional, unique features like behavior-based animation and the ability to turn a project into a template, which is accessible through Final Cut Pro. If you already have Adobe-created artwork, it is easy to import. With Motion, you can bring in elements that you've created in Photoshop and After Effects as well as use Motion's toolset. The graphics can then be easily accessed in the Viewer Window as a template project. This is particularly useful if you need to have a bunch of editors working on your video podcast and not everybody has graphics capabilities.

- **Apple LiveType.** LiveType is a "leftover" application. It comes with Final Cut Express and Final Cut Studio on the

Learning After Effects

After Effects is a relatively expensive piece of software with an enormous feature set. It is not a tool that you can just sit down with and pick up in a few hours. If you're going to spend that much money on a piece of software, do not try to figure out the software on your own. Learning After Effects requires you to spend some time with the program and follow a structured learning regimen. Some of our favorite After Effects learning tools include:

- **After Effects Apprentice** (Trish and Chris Meyer)
- **After Effects @ Work** (Focal Press)
- **Broadcast Graphics on the Spot** (Richard Harrington, Glen Stephens, Chris Vadnais)
- **Creative After Effects** (Angie Taylor)
- **Creative Cow** (www.CreativeCOW.net)
- **Xeler8r** (www.xeler8r.com)

Mac. While it is rudimentary, it does have some nice features. It ships with a large library of graphics assets which makes it easy to produce animated text and backgrounds. While it is really easy to use, you need to be careful not to get sucked into really overused effects.

Technical Issues for Podcasting Graphics

There are several issues when it comes to building still and motion graphics for a podcast. The advice we often hear is specific to podcast graphics. However, if you are inexperienced with broadcast graphics, we strongly recommend additional reading and practice. See the advice in this chapter as being the essential information.

Screen Size and Design Issues

Podcast graphics are usually seen at one of two sizes, 320×240 or 640×480. Neither size is an editing standard in nonlinear editing packages. The closest matches will be the standard definition presets offered by your NLE software. As such we usually build the graphics to match the acquisition format (such as 720×480 in non-square pixels for NTSC and 720×576 in non-square pixels for PAL). We assume that the show is probably going to get reformatted and could end up on a DVD or even be broadcast. Working in standard definition is easy, as that is likely the size at which the video was acquired (if you are working in high definition, then build your graphics to match).

Type Is Good

Be sure to invest in a font for your show that didn't come preinstalled with Microsoft Office. You need to find a visual identity for your podcast, and good use of type is an easy way to do it. Take a look out there; there's a typeface that has your show's personality. Something that is somewhat unique and will help convey the character of your show. Here are a few of our favorite type foundries.

- **Chank** (www.Chank.com)
- **Dinctype** (www.girlswhowearglasses.com)
- **Blue Vinyl** (www.bvfonts.com)
- **Acid Fonts** (www.acidfonts.com)

Also, let us step on our soapbox for a moment. If you're going to use more than one font family, you better have a good reason. If you're going to use more than two fonts, you better have a really good reason. And more than three, you need a note from your mother. Try to limit yourself. You'll see that staying within one family and using different weights creates a polished appearance.

We recommend building your podcast graphics at standard video size, and then editing with your video. You can always resize the entire episode after editing with compression software.

But we usually resize and test our graphics to simulate the podcast environment. No matter which size you deliver, your audience is usually looking at this on a 320 × 240 screen, so don't make them squint. Make the text larger and easier to read. In broadcast graphics, designers usually use a safe title grid that identifies two zones: title safe, which is the innermost 80% of the graphic and where all text should fall; and action safe, which is the innermost 90% and where all essential design elements should fall. In broadcast, if these are ignored, text can become difficult (or even impossible) to read on a television.

The graphic on the left keeps all text within the action-safe zone used by broadcasters (the innermost 90%). In traditional video, text and logo elements are kept within the title-safe area (the innermost 80%), as shown by the graphic on the right.

For podcasting, you can treat the action-safe guides that most graphics programs offer as your title-safe zone. Go all the way out and just leave a 10% margin around the outside edge of the podcasting graphic so the text doesn't get hard to read by being too close to the edge of the computer screen or the edge of the portable media player. By keeping all text within these guides, you ensure that it is easy to read on the portable screen or computer.

However, if your show is going to be used in both traditional and podcasting situations, you may need to create two master sequences for the different graphic standards.

DV Format Production Issues

While the DV format is responsible for making the video production industry significantly more democratic and open, it still has its faults. If you are shooting video using Mini DV, DV Cam, or DVCPRO 25 formats, you are likely using the DV codec in your sequence. This codec is essentially throwing away three-fourths of your graphics information, "smooshing" your graphics to heck. It would be the equivalent of shooting a beautiful photo with your digital camera and then only being able to deliver it at a JPEG set to low quality.

The graphic on the left is an uncompressed original. The one on the right has standard DV compression applied. The differences are subtle, but most evident in the small text details and glowing areas.

There are ways to work around this, however. Some NLEs allow you to mix resolutions in the timeline. Otherwise, what we do is edit the sequence using DV settings (primarily due to the speed of matching sequence settings to the primary camera acquisition format). Then, at the end of the production, we switch our sequence settings to an uncompressed codec for finalizing. This way when you export your self-contained QuickTime movies to compress them for podcast, they come out very clean. The goal with video compression is simple: start high, and finish low. The better quality image you feed into the podcast compression software, the cleaner and smaller file you'll get out.

The digital video codec is the kiss of death to graphics. It instantly throws away three-fourths of the work you've done and makes it look terrible. Be very careful if you're working with DV footage; do not finish your sequences using the DV codec.

Graphic Design Issues for Video Podcasts

Getting your podcast graphics to work great and effectively often comes down to how they are designed. It is important that your graphics are easy to use and modify, as well as look great on their intended playback devices. Here are the key points we've learned when designing graphics for podcasting.

Flexibility

It is essential that your graphics be easy to modify. This can be accomplished in two ways. The first method involves pre-rendering elements and adding them to a template sequence. Essentially everything except the text or media placeholder (for a headshot or video) is rendered in advance. For example, in our weekly shows we only need to add the title and host's name. This makes changes simple and results in a short render time (often done by the video editor). With easy-to-modify graphics, it is not a challenge when it comes time to pump out 40 graphics for a series.

Two very different shows, same principle in ease of production. By keeping show titles easy to modify, you will save significant time in producing custom graphics.

The other technique involves creating edit points right within your graphics. In almost all of our podcast graphics, we find a way to creatively dip to black or dip to a color. This makes it easy to edit the show title or attach it to the body sequence. This has several ramifications, including ease of use and re-branding.

On several shows, we have had to go back to our library of previously edited shows and simply copy and paste the new graphics onto the front using QuickTime Player. We know that we will change the look of graphics packages from time to time in order to refresh our content. We don't want to have old graphics in our podcast feed because it sends an inconsistent message. The lesson learned is that you want to make it easy for graphics to be stitched on. Make sure your graphics are very easy to take on and off of your show. Another lesson learned the hard way: save graphics-free masters of your podcasts so you can easily add new graphics.

This show's graphics were created on a very tight budget and in very little time. Simplicity was the goal all around, and it resulted in a clean and popular appearance. This show was time limited, but spiked as high as number two in the Technology category on iTunes.

Clean Appearance

While clean is a subjective judgment, it is still essential. By *clean*, we mean crisp, easy-to-read, and easy-to-understand designs. You want clarity with your podcast graphics; if things feel too busy, it's probably too busy. If you think it's a little hard to read, your audience will think it's very hard to read. We are not advocating for vanilla design; just remember that podcasting is a very low-resolution medium that is also heavily compressed. You have less latitude than print (and even video), so it is essential you design with the medium in mind.

Match the Style of the Show

The goal is simple: You want the personality of your graphics package to match the style of your show and its host. Make sure that you're figuring out a way to make your show different than the rest. Analyze your perceived competition and develop graphics with a unique appearance that matches your show.

For the Final Cut Help podcast series, the graphic identity is carried through the show's open and sequence graphics onto the set. In fact, the branding and design carries through to the commercial DVDs that are sold by the show's sponsor VASST.

We often see podcast graphics that are "hot and sizzling" and the talent is barely a "warm fish." There is nothing wrong with having low-key or subdued talent, just make sure the graphics match the show's personality. If your show is warm and nurturing, then look to things like the Oxygen or Food Network for graphic ideas and not MTV2.

Style in Action

At RHED Pixel, we produce two weekly shows on Adobe Photoshop. The first show, Understanding Adobe Photoshop, targets a mass appeal audience that is less experienced with the software. The second, Photoshop for Video, takes a look at the software for experienced video professionals and motion graphic artists. Same subject, same host ... different audiences, different graphics.

As such, we re-branded our shows to make them feel very different. The Understanding Adobe Photoshop show is packaged to feel very consumer friendly. Because we were attracting a more basic audience we wanted the opening to feel more like a McDonalds commercial. For the other show, Photoshop for Video, we used a much more aggressive and gritty approach. There are several elements that are very technical, including old registration patterns and testing bars. The graphics would be fairly meaningless except to those in the know. This podcast goes after a niche audience, and the graphics reflect that.

Who are You? Production Company Credit

We are big proponents of following broadcast standards. At the end of nearly all network programming is the production company logo. We always try to place our logo at the end of programs we work on (at bare minimum, our company's name in the show credits). We make the argument that it's just like a broadcast TV show, where you see the production company logo at the end. In our minds, this adds a professional feeling to the entire package, and it is certainly a benefit to the production company.

You should also have a color palette that carries through from graphics to the set. You can take the key colors of your graphics package and repeat them on the video shoot. This looks very good and adds a level of professionalism to the show's appearance.

Consistency in Style

We see many shows that have a patchwork-quilt appearance. This is because different designers often develop the show's graphics in stages. Another contributing factor is that many podcasters rely on stock graphics and then pick and choose from several different volumes or collections. Think of a podcast as being a unique individual; you want it to stand out from the crowd, but not because it is wearing two different colored socks, a fur hat, a leather cowboy jacket, and a Scottish kilt. Make sure your elements match or complement each other so the show remains consistent in its style.

Contrast Test

With podcasting graphics, contrast is key. Does the graphic still work when you remove color? If it does, this means that you have proper contrast and you are ensuring that your audience has an easier time comprehending the information.

How does the graphic hold up when you remove color and just look at contrast? The middle of this animation looks a little low contrast, but where it really matters for the end sponsor logo, contrast is proper.

You'll want to check your graphics in grayscale mode. If they're still easy to read, then they're easy to read. One way to do this is to add an adjustment layer in your graphics application with a hue/saturation effect. By pulling down the saturation, you can strip out the color. Another way to accomplish this is print them out in grayscale mode to a printer. These are both simple, but good tests. If the graphics hold up, then you've got a good balance of contrast and luminance. Proper contrast is essential as it affects how easily the viewer can comprehend the information.

Busyness of Background to Foreground

In recent years, the evolution of the stock animation market has led to a terrible problem. In the quest to stand out from their competition, several manufacturers of stock animation have made their backgrounds more and more elaborate. As such, we've gotten to the point where backgrounds are too busy and compete for attention with foreground elements such as text. A background is just that, a background. We find an easy solution is to blur and darken our backgrounds.

For this video, it was important to find the right balance for the background images. The client wanted to create an active virtual world, but also communicate several ideas.

Another technique we like to use on both our graphics and footage is a vignette effect. This is often called a "power window" and it works very well on the smaller screen since it draws the viewer's attention to the middle. This can be done using a Photoshop file that you lay on top. It also can be accomplished with filters in an NLE. Give it a try, as it helps give your graphics a focal point. You'll find a sample vignette file at www. VidPodcaster.com.

Sticker Shock

Unfortunately, most clients have a very poor understanding of what it takes to make good graphics (we find that client's misperceptions on graphic costs are second only to web design). In this day and age, people will see really cool graphics on somebody else's show and say, "I want it just to look like that." However, they have no concept of what "that" might cost.

It is common to elicit "sticker shock" when you talk to people about graphics, especially because podcasting is a price-sensitive medium. It's important to look for efficiencies in your graphics package (such as the reuse value and ease of modification). Nearly everyone is trying to create podcasts as affordably as possible, because podcasting has caught a lot of people off guard (in other words, no budget). Look to bury your graphics costs and consider spreading the cost out across multiple jobs if the client looks to have an ongoing series. After all, you will want the podcasts to look their best as you build up your portfolio.

Type-on-Pattern Issues

Related to both the contrast and busyness of the image is the type-on-pattern issue-. What often happens in video is that text is placed over a busy or moving background. As such, white text can intersect with a bright area in the background and become very difficult to read. This problem is easy to address.

The use of a solid bar helps the text stand out to the podcast viewer (even when viewed at a small size). The use of uppercase letters was a stylistic choice, but it also helped readability and kept the text blocks more compact. Finally, a drop shadow was added to some elements (such as the logo) to address the moving background.

First make sure that your font choice is relatively thick. A heavier font will hold up better on the video screen. Then add a contrasting edge such as a stroke or drop shadow. Light text should get a dark edge, while dark text should get a light edge. Take advantage of contrasting edges to make the text easier to read.

Additionally, try to keep lines of text shorter. This is because of how podcasts are viewed. On the small screen of an iPod, larger text in smaller blocks is easier to read. A viewer watching on a laptop may blow the video up to full screen. In this case it's going to get pixilated. If the font is thicker and has contrast, it won't fall apart as badly. Fortunately, these guidelines work well for both viewing scenarios. In a confluence of circumstances, thicker, larger text generally holds up better.

Read Time

Many motion graphic designers and editors seem to forget that graphics are actually meant to be read by an audience. The idea with read times is that you want to be able to read the graphic out loud, preferably twice before removing the graphic. This is an old broadcast standard for a good reason.

Unfortunately, most motion graphic designers are watching their motion graphics play back at less than real-time speed. Instead, they just choose an arbitrary number like three seconds. Remember you are adding graphics to add understanding for the viewer. Allowing the graphic to be read aloud twice ensures that the viewer has enough time to read the graphic while still absorbing the other information being presented simultaneously by the host or *B Roll*.

With animated sequences, the read-aloud rule still applies. Be sure each element can be fully understood by your audience by giving it enough time to be easily read twice, out loud.

Music for Podcasts

Finding the right music to use in a podcast is very tricky. Sure, you have the same selection challenges as any video making the music fit the mood—but it goes well beyond that. The biggest challenges are usually legal and licensing. With podcasts, you have all sorts of issues: first the files are shown on the web (which is usually considered worldwide distribution), then add the fact that the items can be downloaded to a user's computer. When it comes to licensing music, things can be very expensive. A few approaches to staying legal are worth considering.

Make a Better Show Graphic

Whether a show is an audio or video podcast, it needs a show logo. This logo is used in the podcast directory services and can also appear in the user's podcasting client software or portable media player. The graphic is usually square and is often displayed at a small size. The RSS spec allows for the graphic to be up to 400 × 400 pixels (but iTunes uses a maximum of 300 × 300 pixels).

Normally, we recommend designing podcast show graphics at 900 × 900 pixels. This way the graphics will be large enough to use on banner graphics on the web or even in small print. Plus when you're looking at it on the computer screen during design, you're not getting a migraine headache because you're staring at a "postage stamp" for hours.

When done, simply invoke Photoshop's Save for Web command (File > Save for Web and Devices). This way you can tell the graphic to 300 × 300 pixels. Then look at it to see whether the text has become hard to read … does the graphic look too busy? It's also a good idea to test at 150 × 150 as well to account for browsing in the iTunes Store.

Buy Out Music

There are several manufacturers of stock music that offer buy-out licenses. Depending on the manufacturer, these might be by track, by disc, or by collection. A simple web search will provide many choices. The key is to spend a little time digging as many of the cheapest and most visible libraries are often the most used. This is still a very good option and will generate a solution with very little effort.

Websites, such as IODA Promonet offer free music to podcasters. Many bands and labels make music available free of charge in exchange for proper recognition in the show or credits.

Pod-Safe Music

Many independent musicians make their music available for promotional reasons. There are websites where musicians of all genres offer up their music for free use as long as you identify them in your show credits. This is a great way to find music that sounds fresh and costs literally nothing.

- **PodSafe Music** (www.podsafemusicnetwork.com)
- **IODA Promonet** (www.promonet.iodalliance.com)
- **Mobygratis** (www.mobygratis.com)
- **AudioFeeds.org** (www.audiofeeds.org)
- **Kahvi Collective** (www.kahvi.org)

Loop-Based Scoring

Building your own music track is much easier with several of the software tools on the market. With products like Apple Soundtrack Pro, Sony Acid, or Adobe Soundbooth, you can arrange your own music to match the duration and mood of your video. The major benefit of these programs is that you can create your own music or arrangements, which are free of any web use restrictions. As an added benefit, the music can be made to work nearly as well as a custom score.

Most of these programs work with musical loops, which are not a continuous song, but rather a single instrument piece. A loop might be a drumbeat or a guitar riff, so you're actually arranging music, using pieces of instrumentals and sounds to create a full song. Loops are usually searchable by duration, key, and style. While a true music background is helpful, many users can still build their own music beds successfully.

Additionally, many famous musicians have their own loops for sale released through Sony and Advanced Media Group. These musicians have opened up either songs or sessions that they've done and make the loops available for free and clear use. Now you pay about $150 for a pack of these, but it's a great way to get a nice sound to your piece. Plus we'd rather pay that once than face legal repercussions for not using music properly.

Original Music Scoring

Don't forget that the world is filled with composers, many of whom are talented and reasonably priced. If we are working on a podcast series that has a reasonable budget, a custom-scored jingle package can work well. You generally will want a short opening theme (usually 20 to 45 seconds) and a few stingers or transitions in the body of the show. While rates will vary per market and composer, this is still a reasonably priced option since you don't need a lot of music created. You can hire a local composer to make a jingle package for you for $750 to $2000, with the buyout rights.

You can usually negotiate a lower price by giving the project an extended timeline. If you give the composer a few weeks' time, he or she can fit your work in between other jobs. You can also offer the composer an end credit in the podcast. Don't undermine the value of a podcast for exposure.

PRO*file*: DC Derby

The DC Derby podcast (www.dcderby.tv) offers coverage of the DC Rollergirls, a league of four roller derby teams that compete in the Washington DC area. Competitive roller derby is on the rise, with nearly 50 leagues around the United States joined under the Women's Flat Track Derby Association. The action is fast and the sport is popular for its athleticism.

Podcaster Michael Tolosa produces video highlights of matches. He also posts interviews with skaters and gets behind-the-scenes footage of the competition. Tolosa chose roller derby because he thought it was both entertaining and appealing to a niche group.

"I've always been a big fan of creating and watching short, entertaining videos. When I found out there were a lot of independently produced shows available through iTunes, I immediately subscribed to about 60 shows," says Tolosa. "It didn't take long before I wanted to produce some podcasts of my own. Six months after being introduced to the world of podcasting, I published the first episode of DC Derby."

Tolosa, a film major with a history of analog video production, saw podcasting as an opportunity to learn digital video filmmaking.

He purchased a high-end HD camera and professional video-editing software and taught himself how to use them. Although Tolosa is new to podcasting, he's learned a few important lessons already.

"Get your first episode published as quickly as possible. It takes awhile just to learn the whole process of getting your first episode published. You have to learn about web hosting, compression settings, RSS feeds, etc. By the time you've taken one episode 'live,' you've already learned just about everything you need to know," Tolosa explains. "It doesn't matter how good your first episode is. Consider it a 'burner' episode. You need to learn the publishing process first. Then you can work on improving the quality of your show. Plus, getting one episode out of the way is like breaking the ice. You won't be as anxious about publishing your next, real episode."

The first episodes were harder than he expected, but now Tolosa is starting to hit his stride.

"I upgraded to a professional digital HD camcorder prior to filming the first episode of my podcast, but wasn't used to all the professional audio settings. For the first two episodes, I only had audio coming through one speaker. After sitting down with

the camera manual for about an hour, I figured out what was wrong with my mic settings," says Tolosa. "Even though the first couple of episodes weren't perfect, I'm glad I went ahead and started podcasting prior to knowing every single setting on the camera. Don't let preparation keep you from actually doing. Go into creating your first podcast knowing that everything won't be perfect the first time through. Don't try to hit a home run with your first episode. Just get it done. Then continue to learn and improve your skills with the following episodes."

One of the DC Derby podcast's strong points from the beginning has been its great soundtrack. Tolosa knew he wanted powerful music to match the intense action. Since

the DC Derby podcast covers the DC scene, Tolosa uses bands from the DC area.

"Do some research on music royalties prior to using copyrighted music in your podcasts. The RIAA will have your head if you use popular music released by record labels," warns Tolosa. "Instead, contact local unsigned bands in your area and ask them for permission to use their music. It's a win-win situation for you and the artists. You get cool music to legally use in your podcast, and the bands get additional exposure."

Gear List

- Canon XH-A1 digital HD camcorder
- Sennheiser wireless lavalier microphone
- Tripod and monopod
- Headphones, batteries, HDV tapes, gaff tape, rubber bands

7

EDITING CONSIDERATIONS

The advent of nonlinear editing (NLE) software has dramatically changed the way video is made. In fact, the emergence of lower-cost (yet powerful) editing tools is directly responsible for the rise of video podcasting. Without a means to create video for the masses, there would be no podcasting. But finding the right nonlinear editing tool is a tricky game. You will encounter several choices on the market as well as hotly contested platform and manufacturer wars. In this chapter, we will share with you tools that meet the needs of various types of podcasters, as well as identify specific tasks you need to accomplish during the editing stage of your podcasts.

The Evolution of Nonlinear Editing

Nonlinear editing tools have been around for many years. The technology is defined by its ability to access any frame of video loaded onto the system, without needing to shuttle through tape. Using a nonlinear editor, you can assemble video in a word-processing like approach. This means that video can be built in segments, which can be easily reordered or modified at any point in time. This is very different than the traditional tape-based methods that involved meticulously assembling one shot after another by dubbing from one tape to another (with little to no ability for changes).

When you work with a nonlinear editing system, you must transfer material such as video from the camera to a computer hard drive. Some formats of videotape must be digitized, which is why some modern cameras offer tapeless acquisition of material

What's the Big Deal?

The emergence of nonlinear editing allows for nondestructive editing. This means that the original source tapes are not modified during editing. Rather, the editing software records the decisions made by the editor in an edit decision list (or EDL). These files can often be interchanged between editing tools (even from different manufactures). Newer systems use XML-based project files, which can transfer much more data between software tools.

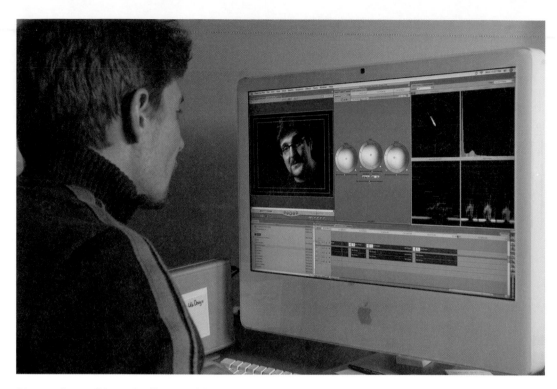

Many nonlinear editing tools offer powerful color correction tools for calibrating and improving images. Software scopes like these used to be a hardware-only option and would add thousands of dollars in cost to an editing system.

FireWire

that can just be transferred. Once the material is imported, it can be edited and arranged using a variety of software tools made by several different companies. Many of these software tools have a rich history and have seen a long period of evolution (see sidebar).

The emergence of DV technology and FireWire signaled a huge shift in the editing marketplace, leading to the release of high-quality tools targeted at significantly broader audiences. Tools like iMovie and Windows Movie Maker brought desktop editing to the homes and schools, while companies like Sony, Avid, Adobe, and Apple released multiple products for different segments of the professional market. Thanks to DV, video could really be edited on fairly standard computers. This revolution in FireWire filmmaking democratized the market. Without this revolution, there would be no video podcasting movement.

A Short History of Nonlinear Editing

The first nonlinear editing system was the CMX 600, which was introduced in 1971 by CMX Systems. The CMX 600 had a console with two black-and-white monitors as well as a light pen to control the system. The system helped establish the idea that the left monitor was where editors made selections and previewed their edits, while the right monitor showed the assembled program. Costing nearly $250,000 (and that is *not* adjusted for inflation), the tool was very expensive and only saw six units placed into use. But it was a start and it led to more innovation.

Many others tried to develop nonlinear editing systems throughout the 1980s. These used computers that coordinated multiple laser discs or several tape recorders. One of the more successful units was the EditDroid system invented by Lucasfilm. Only 24 EditDroid systems were ever produced and the company was eventually sold off to Avid Technology in 1993.

Avid is often seen as the pioneer in nonlinear editing software and hardware. They first showed their Avid/1 product in 1988 to a private audience at a National Association of Broadcasters event. The product continued to evolve with new features. Originally, Avids were intended as an offline tool meant to serve as a creative editing solution; the actual edits would then be reassembled in a linear editing suite (called an online edit).

But as computers and storage technology improved, many industries started building programs on their Avids, then releasing them directly to broadcast. In 1993, a group of industry experts led by a digital video R&D team at the Disney Channel found the key solution. Previously, computers had a storage limit of 50 GB, but these engineers found a way to build a system that gave the Avid Media Composer access to over 7 TB of digital video data. The industry was reinvented again, with feature films now being edited nonlinearly.

These early days were interesting, with lots of innovation and technical challenges. The market saw competition from products like NewTek's Video Toaster and Media 100 editing systems. These both challenged Avid's dominance, mainly by attacking it on price. Other tools emerged such as Adobe Premiere, which offered both software only and a variety of third-party hardware options.

One late entry into the nonlinear editing space is Apple (which is seen by many as a market leader). A group of engineers originally left Adobe to start a project for Macromedia called Keygrip. This project couldn't really get off the ground and was eventually purchased by Apple. It was seen as a way to compete with Adobe Premiere and a precautionary move, since Avid had begun to move away from the Mac platform and push its Windows-based solutions. Final Cut Pro was unveiled in 1999—and was originally not taken very seriously. Apple has continued to invest heavily in the product, however, making major strides in technology and value, leading them to a dominant position in most market segments. A big part of Final Cut Pro's success was the advent of DV-based video formats, which use IEEE 1394 (or FireWire).

NLE Selection Criteria

Asking video pros to tell you which editing system they'd pick will often provoke a very passionate answer. Perhaps it's that editors are often locked away in dark rooms with their tools, but more likely they just have strong feelings about how they like to get their work done. There is no right answer here; rather, you'll

Our Tools of Choice

We think it's important to be transparent here. Both authors have significant experience using nonlinear editing software. We both began using Avid editing systems (in fact Richard has completed both Avid's Master Editor and Certified Instructor programs). When we began RHED Pixel, we chose the Mac platform due to personal experience and our ability to maintain it. RHED Pixel was one of the first companies to adopt Final Cut Pro and use it for a variety of broadcast and non-broadcast projects. We continue to use Avid and have also used Premiere Pro (mainly for its excellent integration with Adobe After Effects). We are open-minded and constantly look at new tools to compare their features and opportunities.

need to balance out your needs and budget. There are some selection criteria that you should be aware of. This advice is framed solely around use in video podcasting, so keep this in mind when you read our recommendations.

Cost

Nonlinear editing tools run the gamut in cost. For example, both iMovie and Windows Movie Maker are included with Apple and Microsoft's operating systems. So if you are looking for a tool at no additional cost, you likely have one. Both of these tools are effective, but many users eventually outgrow them as they develop their video editing skills. In the next category you'll find tools like Apple Final Cut Express for Mac and Adobe Premiere Elements or Sony Vegas Movie Studio. These tools start to increase the feature set for the editor and run between $79 and $299.

But even the pro-level tools can be within reach of a video podcasters. Many choose to invest in options like Final Cut Studio from Apple or Production Premium from Adobe. These bundles offer significant savings and are useful as they combine video editing, motion graphics, sound editing, and encoding tools into one bundle.

Be sure to fully explore the tools and their costs. It's a good idea to visit a certified reseller or approach peers so you can try out

Nonlinear Editing Software

There are lots of tools used to edit video. Selecting the right one involves balancing several factors. If you are considering investing in new nonlinear editing software, be sure to evaluate these options. We have listed tools by top manufacturers, sorted alphabetically by manufacturer, then by cost. There are more tools on the market; these are just the most popular in the video podcasting space.

Adobe Systems (www.adobe.com)
- Adobe Premiere Elements (Microsoft Windows)
- Adobe Premiere Pro (Microsoft Windows, Mac OS X)

Apple Inc. (www.apple.com)
- iMovie (Mac OS X)
- Final Cut Express (Mac OS X)
- Final Cut Pro (Mac OS X)

Avid Technology (www.avid.com)
- Avid Liquid (Microsoft Windows)
- Avid Xpress Pro (Microsoft Windows, Mac OS X)
- Avid Media Composer (Microsoft Windows, Mac OS X)

Media 100 (www.media100.com)
- Media 100 HDe (Mac OS X)
- Media 100 SDe (Mac OS X)

Microsoft (www.microsoft.com)
- Windows Movie Maker (Microsoft Windows)

Sony (www.sonycreativesoftware.com)
- Vegas Movie Studio (Microsoft Windows)
- Vegas (Microsoft Windows)

Premiere Elements is a flexible tool that is works well-suited for DV and HDV workflows.

the systems you are considering. You can also read video editorial reviews from magazines such as *Layers*, *DV Magazine*, and *Studio Monthly*, where you can get independent opinions on editing software.

Ease of Use

Ease of use is very subjective, and will depend on the individual user. We have heard from many users that Apple, Adobe, and Sony lead the way with products that are powerful and easy to use. It is important to realize, though, that video editing is a complex task. Be prepared to pick up books, watch training DVDs, and even enroll in a class to learn video editing skills. The biggest mistake we see is choosing to go it alone and teach yourself. Sure, you probably could have learned to drive a car with no

Apple iMovie offers an easy-to-use interface and is designed for newcomers to nonlinear editing.

outside help, but it would get really expensive with all the accidents. Same holds true with video editing … if you are going to invest in expensive equipment, invest time and money in learning to get the most out of that gear.

Editing Formats

Not every NLE can edit every type of video format. For example, while iMovie can work with the HDV video format, it cannot work with more professional forms of HD such as DVCPRO HD or XDCAM. Different camera manufacturers have closer ties to certain NLEs, so be sure to investigate if your type of camera or video deck will work with a particular NLE. It's important that you fully explore this important connection before investing money in technology. A good place to start is to look at the manufacturers' web pages and see which equipment and video formats they list as supported.

Additionally, we prefer resolution-independent NLEs. Tools such as Adobe Premiere Pro, Apple Final Cut Pro, and Sony Vegas allow you to bring in a variety of materials and mix them in one

Slated Takes

 We have already discussed using a slate to sync and mark takes when in the field. Be sure the editor knows to look for these (and that whoever is loading the footage doesn't chop them off). This way, people not involved in the shooting process can edit the podcasts.

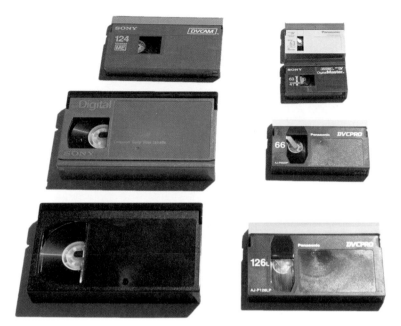

timeline. This is particularly useful if you need to frequently work with photos or screen captures.

For example, our Photoshop for Video podcast takes video shot on an SD video camera with non-square pixels and intercut it with screen captures that are digitally acquired. The screen captures are generally larger (often much more) as we can then pan around and show close-ups of the software interface (we simply scale down to show the whole user interface). We prefer this flexibility as it increases our working options.

Multi-Camera Editing Abilities

The ability to synchronize and edit multi-camera video shoots is essential to video podcasting. When executed properly, a multi-camera shoot saves enormous time in the postproduction process. Once the angles are synchronized, it is easy to maintain continuity. Additionally, the material is easier to edit because you have multiple angles and can cut between them with a single keystroke. Multi-camera options are available for most pro-level tools:

- Adobe Premiere Pro
- Apple Final Cut Pro
- Avid Xpress Pro and Media Composer
- Sony Vegas

Export Abilities

Just as important as what you can put into an NLE is what you can get out. Most nonlinear editing tools fully support MPEG-4 video. Some build support right into the application via the export menu, while others tie their products to a third-party tool such as Sorenson Squeeze. It's important that you test the abilities of the NLE to make an MPEG-4 video file for use in video podcasting. While many editing tools do an adequate job, you may still consider some of the dedicated compression tools that we will discuss in Chapter 8.

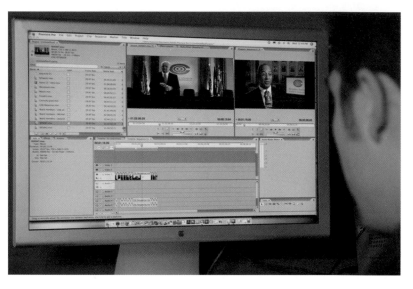

Adobe Premiere Pro offers a great variety of export options, including Flash, DVD, Windows Media, and, of course, podcast-ready MPEG-4 files.

Customer Support

As we've said many times, editing video is not easy. Therefore, you'll want to examine how much support is available for a product. Look on the company's website for an active user forum. Does the company offer certified training classes? How many books or DVDs on the tool have been published? Can you find a local user's group in your area for sharing ideas and support? Different manufacturers have different levels of loyalty. Apple and Sony tend to have the most zealots followed by broad support for Adobe tools and a large, established training system for Avid.

Technical Considerations During Editing

The editing stage is the place where all the pieces come together into the final story. In many ways, it all comes down to how the editor puts the pieces together. It is beyond the scope of this book to teach you how to edit (although we have lots of recommended resources on the book's website). Rather, we'll identify the most common problem areas when it comes to editing video podcasts. These are the skills you must master (or find someone who has). Knowing what problems to watch for is the hardest thing. Here's what we've learned (often the hard way).

Determining Finishing Size

There is often debate as to how to set up your sequences for editing. Some suggest setting the sequences to match the finished podcast size. While this is a valid choice, we usually don't follow this method. Working with non-standard frame sizes usually results in significantly more editing and rendering. After all, it is easy enough to reformat the video when it is edited (more on this in the next chapter).

The best advice here is to set your video editing timeline to match your primary acquisition source of video. This means that if you shot DV NTSC, set your timeline to 720 × 480 non-square pixels. It is also a *very* good idea to stick with the sequence presets that ship with your editing software. Just be sure to match the right sequence settings to your footage. If you have to render everything in your timeline, the sequence settings are wrong.

Determining Sequence Settings

It is important to set up your NLE timeline properly; otherwise the settings could lower the quality of your images. With a podcast, determining the right sequence setting to use can be a bit tricky. This is because podcasts often mix elements like video, archival material, photos, and screen captures. The guiding factor is the format of your primary source material. You want your editing sequence to match your most dominant or important source.

This generally means that you want to set your sequence to match your on-camera footage. The good news is that most NLE software tools make this easy. It is generally best to set your sequence up to match your camera footage so you get the most real-time performance from the computer and can edit without first having to render.

A Camera Is Not a Deck

We see many people plug their cameras in to load material into their video editing systems. This is a *very bad idea*, as it significantly stresses the equipment. Shuttling and rewinding tape can quickly wear out a camera. You are much better off buying a tape deck to feed your material. This way you can have shooting and editing going simultaneously and your camera investment should last significantly longer.

Apple's Final Cut Pro offers very flexible sequence settings. These allow you to create very customized sequences to match nonstandard footage.

After the initial edit is complete, you need to evaluate your image quality. If your sequence contains DV footage mixed with higher-quality sources like screen captures or photos that use less compression, you'll want to "up-rez" your sequence. Duplicate your edited sequence, then modify its compression type (or codec) to match your highest-quality material (such as Animation, Avid 1:1, or Apple 8-bit). You'll likely need to render the entire sequence, but this file will make a much better source for compression.

Maintaining Optimal Color and Exposure

Many podcasters understand little about color correcting their video. This is because web video doesn't have the same rigorous issues of quality control as broadcast video. This doesn't mean that you should ignore the stricter rules of broadcast television.

- Video codecs work best when the source material has its colors and exposure set properly.
- You might also need to deliver your video for playback on a television.
- Following the best practices of video is literally good practice, and will make all of the videos you do look more professional.

You want to make sure that you have adjusted exposure properly. Try to avoid blowing the image out. If it's a choice between too light or too dark, favor a little bit dark. Make sure you have sufficient contrasts because a lack of contrast will cause problems when you compress.

Most modern video editing systems include reasonably good tools for color correction. The problem is that most NLEs contain bad tools as well. In general, look for three-way color correctors or curves-based color tools. On the other hand, never use brightness or contrast filters, as they are the two worst filters for fixing video images. Color correction is a tricky task; be sure to invest in some training to learn which tools work best for your NLE.

Color Grading for Best Look

Color grading goes beyond mere color correction. It is the manipulation of color for artistic purposes. You'll often choose to manipulate the color in your podcast to help give it a visual identity. The manipulation of color is a very powerful way to convey mood and style to your audience.

There are several third-party tools that are useful for manipulating color in your video. These plug-ins cost extra but offer powerful options that can simulate film as well as processing techniques used in cinema. While you may not be able to do color grade on every show, download and try out some of the following tools:

- **Magic Bullet Suite** (www.redgiantsoftware.com)—Final Cut Pro, Premiere Pro, Avid
- **Nattress Film Effects** (www.nattress.com)—Final Cut Pro
- **Celluloid Film Looks** (www.vasst.com)—Sony Vegas
- **Tiffen Dfx Software** (www.tiffen.com)—Final Cut Pro, Premiere Pro, Avid

Color Correction Training

Looking for training on color correction? Be sure to check out www.vasst.com. They offer training DVDs on Adobe, Apple, Avid, and Sony.

Using Color to Tell a Story

If you're looking for more on using color in your video productions, be sure to check out *The Visual Story* by Bruce Block or *If it's Purple, Someone's Gonna Die* by Patti Bellantoni.

Check for Flash Frames

Keep Getting Flash Frames?

 Do you keep ending up with flash frames in your edits? The likely culprit is you! It is a bad idea to drag video to or around your timeline. It is a very inaccurate way to edit and often results in "little" errors due to sloppy dragging. Instead you should use the precise trimming controls as well as In and Out points for your initial edits.

Before we export a show for use as a podcast, we give it a thorough scouring. One of the things to check includes looking for flash frames. A flash frame is usually a one- or two-frame edit that is unintentional. It may be a few frames from a scene change or a small gap where no video is present.

It sounds meticulous, but step through your show and review each edit point. You can often find a keyboard command to cycle around your edit points playing a few seconds before and after. The quest for flash frames is ingrained in Richard's head thanks to an influential professor named John Lytle. Trust us: Avoid flash frames … they are amateurish.

Consider Transitions Carefully

You will want to carefully consider the use of wipes and transitions in your podcasts. Oftentimes transitions will "break up" due to a podcast's compression. A transition (especially a dissolve) is much more complex to effectively compress. This is because so many of the pixels are changing at the same time and usually quite rapidly.

Podcast compression relies on MPEG-4 technology, which is based on saving space by updating only the pixels that change. A wipe causes a spike in the data needed to show the image clearly. Because podcasts generally have caps on their data rates, this results in the picture breaking up. Many podcasters eliminate wipes altogether and instead rely on the most basic dissolves and fade-to-color transitions (or even the most basic transition of all—the cut).

Avid editing systems offer several transition styles to choose from.

Bad Dissolves and Transitions

It's very easy to get flash frames in your transitions. They can be caused by a shot change at the end of your clip. This happens a lot when previously edited material or items that were sloppily logged and captured are edited together.

It's not your fault really; you can't always know that a transition will use parts of the clip you couldn't see when you started the edit.

1. The easiest way to check this is to enter trim edit mode. Double-click an edit to enter trim mode at a particular edit.
2. Press the space bar to review the edit. Watch it closely, looking for a scene change mid-transition. Often a one- or two-frame roll edit will solve the problem and not change the feel of the show.
3. Move to the next edit in your timeline and check it as well.
4. Repeat for each edit.

Dealing with Interlaced Material

There's a very good chance that the video in your timeline is interlaced (even if it is shot 24p). Most video formats involve some interlacing. This technology is leftover from the earliest days of television. Video interlacing causes half of one frame to load, followed by the second half. This material is often identified as upper or lower field (or even and odd). Essentially, every other frame of video is refreshed each 1/60th of a second for NTSC video and every 1/50th of a second for PAL.

Dual Chain Errors

 If you are using both FireWire hard drives and a camera or deck, you can have major technical problems. For most machines, the built-in FireWire ports all share the same system bus. This leads to major problems when you try to load video into the system and write it out to drives at the same time. The solution is either to capture to a second, high-speed internal drive or to hook up an additional FireWire card. This can often be added to an empty card slot in a tower or slipped into a cardbus slot on a laptop. These options will run you between $50 and $100, and will significantly cut down on technical issues like dropped frame and aborted capture errors.

The frame on the left shows how interlacing can affect image quality when viewed on a non-interlaced display (such as a computer or portable media player). The frame on the right was shot progressive with a Panasonic DVX-100B.

Power Windows: Simple Vignettes

 In the traditional teleceine process where film is transferred to video for editing, the colorist often adds a vignette (or power window) to the footage. Vignettes are a simple way to draw a viewer's attention subtly to a person's face or some other object on screen. Most NLEs offer a vignette plug-in. You can also find a free vignette overlay file on this chapter's page at www.VidPodcaster.com.

Spelling Errors

We'll let you in on a cold, hard fact. If there are spelling errors in a show, it's always the editor's fault. It doesn't matter where the errors came from, whether it was the client or producer; it's still the editor's fault. Through the years we have built up a constant paranoia. There will be spelling mistakes; therefore, scrub your graphics carefully and look for errors. Every time we forget our own advice, the phone rings or the email chimes … it's a client or viewer letting us know there's an error. Be paranoid, expect problems, and then be thorough in your final quality check.

While this is useful for video that is intended for television sets (it can produce smoother motion), it looks terrible on progressive displays. An interlaced video file is very jagged on a portable media player or computer display. Therefore, you need to determine when to remove interlacing.

- **Shoot Progressive.** If you know that you're only delivering to podcast, try to get rid of fields and shoot your video progressive.
- **De-interlace the Timeline.** If your NLE allows, set your Video Editing timeline to progressive. You'll generally need to remove fields using a plug-in or effect. Most NLEs include a de-interlacer or flicker filter. A better option though is to purchase a re-interlacer and advanced de-interlacer plug-ins. Standouts in this area include Big Box of Tricks for Final Cut Pro (www.nattress.com), FieldsKit for After Effects, Premiere Pro, and Final Cut Pro (www.revisionfx.com), or ReSizer 2.0 for Premiere Pro and Final Cut Pro (www.digitalanarchy.com). Filters can take a while to render, so weigh carefully adding the filters to your edit. We generally recommend filtering during the edit if you want greater control or plan to export several versions of the file.
- **During Compression.** Many compression tools offer the ability to de-interlace via a filter as part of the encode process. This option is valid, but only works well if all the material in the timeline is from consistent sources. If you have mixed many sources in the timeline (such as footage from different cameras), it is often better to de-interlace your footage within the timeline itself via a filter.

Shot Composition

If you have a lot of experience editing video for other, more traditional, mediums, you'll need to retrain yourself a bit. Podcasting involves putting video out to devices that are not usually television sets. As such, the podcasting audience generally sees the traditional underscan area where the outermost 10% is ignored in broadcast. This means you need to choose your shots with the whole frame in mind.

Additionally, with shot composition, you're going to be tighter than you're probably used to. Instead of wide shots, you're more likely to use medium or medium close-up shots. This is because of the lower resolution and smaller size that most podcasts are published in. The best thing for an experienced video creator to do is export and test their podcasts early on. Get used to seeing your video on smaller screens and computer displays. Let this guide you as you select shots to use.

Audio Mix

Your podcast may end up with several tracks of audio. Many editors will try to "troubleshoot" their audio mix. The editors intently listen to their show, as if intensity alone could move the edit from a "fine" cut to a "final" cut. Intense focus is a good thing, but make things a little easier by narrowing your focus.

We generally find that the only way to spot problems is to narrow our focus. Problems will stand out in your audio track when you listen to the elements separately. Use these tips:

- Turn off your audio monitors to listen to tracks (or pairs) individually. This way you can isolate problems with the audio tracks.
- If you've added audio edits to your music, do things transition smoothly, or are you trying to hide your music edits? Learn to use your NLE trimming tools to finesse audio edits.
- Are there any loud breaths, gasps, or "guttural" sounds in your narration or sound bites? Throat clearings and coughs can be easily cleaned up.
- Since many viewers of your podcast will listen with headphones, you should too. This way you get an idea of what the viewer will experience.

Little Upcuts

No matter how good an audio editor you are, the more edits in your vocal tracks, the more likely you are to have small pops in your sound track. We usually add several four- or six-frame audio dissolves to all audio edits on a narration track. These short dissolves go a long way toward smoothing things out in your vocal track.

After adding the dissolves, be sure to listen to your mix. You want to make sure that when you add a dissolve you're not picking up extra audio (random words and double breaths) from the media in the clip's handles.

Using Dynamic Noise Reduction?

Many NLEs offer the ability to use a dynamic noise reduction filter. This technology works by sampling the ambient noise in a shot when people aren't talking. This can then be used to filter out the noise from the scene. While this works great, here's an important piece of advice. Fix any sound problems like this first, before you start to edit. It is much easier to filter and fix the entire interview or on-camera take than it is to go back and do it 15 times since you made several edits. This will save you significant time and effort.

Audio Normalization

Pay attention to the audio levels. The podcasting audience is largely comprised of people with headphones jacked into their ears. If your audio mix keeps varying from very loud to very quiet, you will annoy your audience.

Audio is a much bigger issue when you've got the sound pumped directly into your ears. So a sudden blast because the talent got really loud will cause someone to take the ear buds out and turn your show off. Keep in mind that many people on a podcast are listening to the audio with greater attention and they're used to well-mixed audio music, so they're going to expect a better audio mix.

Fortunately, many NLEs or bundled audio editors offer normalization gain. This process attempts to automatically smooth out your audio levels. It won't totally "flatten" the mix, but it will move it all closer to the middle. Your highest highs will drop to a specified target (in decibels) and your lows will be raised closer to the center. This is a very important step and worth doing.

Run Time Strategies

Never forget your target run time. For most podcasts, you are editing short-form entertainment or training. It is far better to keep a podcast short and to the point. In our opinion, this is an easy way to meet the audience's needs and to lower production costs.

There's not much difference in the audience's mind between 15 minutes of content that is delivered in three 5-minute chunks or in one 15-minute episode. For the audience, it generally has the same perceived value (15 minutes' worth).

Keep an Eye on the Finish Line

Here's a suggested workflow to improve the quality of your podcasts. These steps should be completed in order and are based on a professional video workflow. The checklist can, of course, be amended with project-specific tasks, but here is a general list that you can adapt for your needs. (Thanks to Robbie Carman for the suggestion.)

1. Watch the show.
2. Note problems with video and audio using markers.
3. Color correct the show.
4. Mix the show's audio track.
5. Check graphics for consistency (e.g., fonts, colors, position, and spelling).
6. Watch and get approval for the show.
7. Output the show and create compressed files.
8. Archive and back up the show.

The difference is to whoever is funding the show. You are financially better off if you can generate more episodes with less work. You'll do much better by thinking shorter and getting more individual episodes. This is actually what most audiences prefer—people favor shorter content with podcasting because they are consuming it as shorter, on-demand content.

Be sure you monitor your podcast and agree on a target length. For example, you may determine that you want all episodes to run between 4 and 6 minutes. But if the show inched closer to 7 or 8 minutes, you'd split it in into two parts. If the show clocked in at 12 minutes, you could deliver two 6-minute episodes or three 4-minute shows. The important logic here is that you pick a target run time, then manage your editing so the segments time out.

One trick is to add a marker in your timeline to make it easier to see your target run time. Remember, most shows benefit from editing out the "bad" parts. A shorter show helps you distill your content to only the best content.

Backup Progress

Save your work … there, we've said it. Having an organized approach to backing up your work is essential. We generally take a multifaceted approach to our backups. Here are a few strong suggestions for implementation in your projects.

- **Drive Mirroring.** If the content we are using is irreplaceable (for example, screen captures or tapeless acquisition

with no tape backup) then we mirror our drive. This involves getting an identical-size or larger drive and copying all of the content from the edit drive. We can recount a few times too many where this basic backup has saved the day. Once the project is done and archived, you can erase and reuse your mirrored drive.

- **Auto-save/Vault/Attic.** Most NLEs offer some level of control of the program's ability to autosave. This means that you can target a set number of automated project backups to be recorded on a different directory from the system drive or media drive. We often specify a removable drive like a USB "thumb" drive for backup.
- **Nightly Backup.** We recommend giving every editor or graphics person involved in the project their own portable hard drive. Additionally, mandate that their project files be backed up every night before leaving work. This is a very good idea ... and puts ownership into the team's hands.
- **Self-Contained Movies.** When you export your movie files for compression, we recommend "self-contained" QuickTime or AVI files. Many users choose "reference" movies, which are dependant on project media and render files. A self-contained file can be easily used in the future if DVD compilation or recompression needs arise. While saving a master copy, be sure to save "clean" versions—without advertisements—so you can repurpose the content later. Hard drives have gotten much cheaper, and the extra effort is great insurance for the future.

- **Project Folder.** We're often asked about our backup strategies. What do we save, where do we store things on our drives? Here's one method that works for us. We create a project template folder. Inside we put folders for all sorts of common media types, such as a sequences folder, a capture folder to hold loaded video, a graphics folder, and an audio folder. Within these folders things are further broken down into source projects, renders, and so on. You will want to create a folder structure that works for you. By using the same structure for each project, you can easily find project assets, as well as make changes. Plus this folder can be easily backed up to a mirrored drive or archived at the end of a project.

8

ENCODING THE PODCAST

Although you may work hard to create a great-looking video, delivering uncompressed video over the Internet is just impractical. Uncompressed video formats can top out at 1 GB per minute, and even DV compression weighs in at 200 MB per minute. This would cost a fortune to deliver and not even the most motivated audience members would be willing to invest the time need to get the content. Fortunately, video compression techniques and technology have dramatically improved. It is now possible to deliver a video that looks great, using data rates of 1–10 MB per minute. However, getting a video to still look great despite discarding 95% or more of the information involves skill, time, and technology. We can help you with two of the three, but when it comes to time you'll have to learn patience or just keep buying faster computers.

Image quality is essential as consumers start to watch podcasts on larger screens. Thanks to Front Row, which is installed on most Macs, many users are watching podcasts full-screen.

The Challenge of Encoding

The task of encoding video faces a triple constraint. In order to come up with the right encoding technique, you must balance file size, ease of development, and final quality. This is not unlike the old adage, "Good, fast, cheap … pick two." Unfortunately, you (and the world) want all three.

- Getting a small file size with good image quality is not easy.
- Likewise, you can usually generate high-quality podcast files quickly using default presets with the encoding tools, but the files will be unnecessarily large.
- Of course, you can make small files quickly by just throwing away information. But these fast encoding methods don't deliver great-looking files.

Before you give up and think this is hopeless, don't worry—we'll get you there. With a little knowledge, common sense, and patience, you can create great-looking files that are ready to podcast.

Determining Delivery Format

You will face some important decisions early on, when you determine your delivery format. For example, making video files that will work on an RSS feed is a lot easier than making files that work on an iPod. And if you want to reach a broader audience (i.e., people who aren't using iTunes) then your list gets a bit narrower. Picking the right format is a give-and-take scenario, so let's explore some of the options.

●	▶ David Lawrence's Personal Netcast	EXPLICIT	MPEG audio file	10:47
●	▼ Digital Heaven – Hot Tips	CLEAN	MPEG-4 video file	
●	☑ Hot Tips – Find in Timeline	🖵	MPEG-4 video file	3:56
●	☑ Hot Tips – Faster Effects Editing	🖵	MPEG-4 video file	2:56
	▼ HD Podcast | washingtonpost.com	SUBSCRIBE		
	▼ KCRW's Good Food Video	SUBSCRIBE	MPEG-4 video file	
	☑ Tomatoes, Grated and Baked – Video Podcast	🖵	MPEG-4 video file	11:00
●	▶ The Land of Nod's Nodcast Podcast		MPEG audio file	20:14
●	▶ Local 101 Official Podcast	SUBSCRIBE	MPEG audio file	16:10
●	▶ Menox Music Mix – Enhanced AAC Feed	SUBSCRIBE	AAC audio file	1:15:57
●	▶ Photoshop CS3 Sneak Peek	CLEAN	MPEG-4 video file	9:30
●	▼ Photoshop for Video	CLEAN	MPEG-4 video file	
●	☑ 49 The Power of Adjustment Layers – Photoshop for Video	🖵	MPEG-4 video file	6:14
●	☑ 48 Fixing Saturation – Photoshop for Video	🖵	MPEG-4 video file	9:22
	☑ 47 Using the Levels Adjustment Part 2 – Photoshop for Video	🖵	MPEG-4 video file	3:58
	☑ 46 Using the Levels Adjustment Part 1 – Photoshop for Video	🖵	MPEG-4 video file	8:19
	☑ 45 Fading Filters – Photoshop for Video	🖵	MPEG-4 video file	5:00

While you'll only see MPEG-4 video file in your podcast browser, there's more to it than that. There are two common forms of video used for podcasts, MPEG-4 part 2 and MPEG-4 part 10 (also called H.264).

File Format

For video podcasts, video is delivered in one of two MPEG-4 formats (which can also be wrapped in a QuickTime .mov container). While you'll encounter *many* other formats used in online video (including YouTube, Flash video, Google video, and Windows Media), they are not all podcasting formats. Don't make the mistake of lumping every single online video file format into podcasting.

MPEG-4

The MPEG-4 format is really a suite of standards with many parts. Each part defines a set of standards for aspects such as audio, video, and file formats. MPEG-4 was first introduced in 1998, but continues to evolve with important new changes. MPEG is an acronym for the ISO/IEC Moving Picture Experts Group, which serves as the governing body for the format.

The two most common parts of MPEG-4 are part 2, which is used in codecs such as DivX and QuickTime 6, and H.264, which is part of QuickTime 7 and high-definition DVDs and Blu-ray discs. We'll explore the newer H.264 in a moment, but let's first look at the common .mp4 file that is often used by podcasters.

Many encoding tools, including Telestream's Episode Pro, offer presets for different encoding jobs. Note that certain players can handle both types of MPEG-4 video, while many newer devices prefer H.264 video.

AVC ... H.264 by Another Name

 Don't be surprised to see yet another name for H.264 codecs, AVC. This term is meant to be a more "consumer-friendly". You'll see this term frequently on different manufacturers products.

Many compression tools offer the more plainly labeled MPEG-4 option. This generally means that the older MPEG-4 part 2 Simple Profile specs are being followed. This ensures greater compatibility with QuickTime 6. The format is also more likely to play using other web-based players such as RealPlayer and the open-source VLC media player. Some podcasters favor this format if they are targeting a user base running older computer operating systems. While the format does offer broader support, it does not offer the same level of quality of the newer H.264 format.

H.264

The H.264 format is an extension of the MPEG family and is also called MPEG-4 part 10, or AVC (Advanced Video Coding). This format is broadly used (outside of podcasting) for broadcast television, HD DVDs, and Blu-ray DVDs. The format was first drafted in 2003, and was adopted globally by 2005. H.264 video wrapped in an MPEG-4 container is the preferred format of Apple and is used for movie trailers on Apple's website and for TV shows and movies available for sale in the iTunes Store.

H.264 Is Future-Proof

With H.264, we seem to have a video format that most manufacturers can agree on. The H.264 format gives excellent quality across multiple bandwidths—from 3G for mobile phones to HD television broadcasts. This is great news as it means there is a lot of support for and effort being spent on tools and technology.

With H.264 being mandatory for HD DVDs and Blu-ray specifications and for 3rd Generation Partnership Project (3GPP) standards, H.264 is going to be around for a long time. Additionally, major manufacturers like Apple, Sony, Nokia, Palm, Blackberry, and even Microsoft are on board.

If your content has an eye to the future, stick with H.264.

Sony's PlayStation Portable (PSP) device is a popular because it combines a portable media player with a gaming console. Besides its ability to play movies and games, the PSP includes an integrated web browser and offers users the ability to sync or subscribe to podcasts. In fact, in some parts of the world, you can add a Go!Cam video camera to the PSP to record video, and then edit, compress, and upload right from the PSP.

Support for H.264 extends beyond Apple. In 2005, Sony added complete support to the PSP line. In 2006, Microsoft launched the Zune portable media player, which included both MPEG-4 and H.264 support. In 2007, YouTube began encoding all uploaded videos to both their standard player and H.264. This move broadened the reach of YouTube videos to both the iPhone and iPod Touch models. Additionally, Adobe Media Player released in 2008 also supports H.264 in addition to Flash video.

The format was brought to life as a way of providing "DVD quality" at half the data rate (i.e., file size) of optical discs. The format specs mandated that, besides being of smaller file size, the format should be relatively easy to use, not cost-prohibitive, and able to work on devices from many manufacturers. The format has succeeded and is the ideal choice for most video podcasters.

MOV

You will occasionally encounter a podcast that uses the .mov format. While this is possible, it is not as good a choice. The .mov format is simply a container format and supports many codecs, including those using MPEG-4. However, the .mov implementation offers reduced compatibility.

Screen Size

If you intend your podcast files to work on portable media players, you can have two frame sizes; it can be 640 × 480 or 320 × 240. If a podcast is intended for playback on devices like a laptop or an AppleTV, then HD resolutions up to 1280 × 720 are possible.

Before you decide on a delivery size, however, you need to analyze your target audience and their technological makeup. Keep an eye on how big your files are getting; you'll eventually reach a threshold of customers' willingness to download. How big can the file get? Will people complain that the image quality doesn't look good or will they complain that it takes too long to download?

Data Rate

The image quality of a podcast is strongly affected by the data rate of the podcast file. Higher data rates generally mean better image quality, but they can also increase the amount of hardware needed to play back the file. The data rate really becomes an issue when portable media players are involved. The larger data rate files won't work on most portable media players, as they don't contain the required processing power to play back higher data rates. Additionally, larger data rates put a greater demand on power, which drains batteries quickly.

Data rate is often described in kilobits per second (kbps) or the larger megabits per second (Mbps). These numbers are generally specified in the compression software and impact the total size of the file.

Delivering Podcasts with Apple Compatibility

For most podcasters, compatibility with an iPod is an essential requirement. While an iPod is not the only way your audience will consume your podcast, it is still a very popular method.

Therefore, you'll want your files to work on Apple's portable media players.

The Apple iPod and the iPhone support video up to 640 × 480. If you are targeting Apple TV for HD playback, you can use a video file up to 1280 × 720. You can ensure compatibility with iPods and iPhones using the following guidelines:

- H.264 video, up to 1.5 Mbps, 640 × 480, 30 fps, low-complexity version of the Baseline Profile with AAC-LC audio up to 160 kbps, 48 kHz, stereo audio in .m4v, .mp4, and .mov file formats
- H.264 video, up to 768 kbps, 320 × 240, 30 fps, Baseline Profile up to Level 1.3 with AAC-LC audio up to 160 kbps, 48 kHz, stereo audio in .m4v, .mp4, and .mov file formats
- MPEG-4 video, up to 2.5 Mbps, 640 × 480, 30 fps, Simple Profile with AAC-LC audio up to 160 kbps, 48 kHz, stereo audio in .m4v, .mp4, and .mov file formats

If you are podcasting HD video, you are likely targeting computers and television sets. In this case, it is a good idea to use the Apple TV guidelines. The Apple TV unit is designed as an easy way for consumers to play media from their personal computers on their televisions or home entertainment systems. You can ensure compatibility with Apple TV using the following guidelines:

- H.264 video, up to 5 Mbps, 1280 × 720, 24 fps, Progressive Main Profile. Apple TV supports AAC-LC audio up to 320 kbps.

Looking to Put 16:9 Video on an iPod?

If you need to put 16:9 video on an iPod or iPhone, you'll need to keep the video within the 640 pixel width constraint. The correct size for a 16:9 video file, therefore, is 640 × 360 pixels.

Apple TV Video Specifications

Input	Output
640 × 480, 30 fps	640 × 480, 30 fps, 3 Mbps*
1280 × 720, 24 fps	1280 × 720, 24p 5 Mbps*
1280 × 720, 30 fps	960 × 540, 30 fps 4 Mbps*
1920 × 1080, 24 fps	1280 × 720, 24 fps 5 Mbps*
1920 × 1080, 30 fps	960 × 540, 30 fps 4 Mbps*
1080i up to 60 fps	960 × 540, 30 fps 4 Mbps*

*Represents an average bit rate.

If you want to create a single file that works on all three technologies, then deliver a 640 × 480 file and keep the data rate below 1.5 Mbps.

What About Alternate Delivery?

While we firmly believe that podcasting is the best way to effectively reach the broadest audience, it's not a bad idea to try multiple delivery techniques. By releasing your content in multiple formats, you can reach more people.

While a broad approach seems logical, there are a few risks with alternativee delivery approaches. Using more than one format adds additional costs to both the compression and the hosting stages. Your podcast ranking can also suffer because your customer base is spread across multiple channels. There are a number of ways to deliver web video; let's explore how these can be used in conjunction with your podcasting efforts.

MacBreak is produced by Pixel Corps in HD. The show is then distributed at three different sizes to best serve its diverse audience.

Split Feeds

If you want to deliver a podcast at multiple sizes, split your podcast feed into multiple parts. Rather than sticking multiple sizes in one feed, you're better off delivering the podcast as two or more feeds. For example, you may want to deliver a 320 × 240 podcast for faster download times, but also offer the larger 640 × 480 size to meet customer requests.

With this option you simply create a feed for each format. This way a customer can choose to subscribe for only the size video they want. Split feeds are a great way to service customers, but they do add extra work for the podcaster.

Flash Video

Many web developers favor Flash video since it supports both interactivity and tight integration with a website's user interface. Flash video options work very well for embedded players. These can be added easily to blogs or other websites. These embedded players can be used as a way to introduce your web-browsing audience to the world of podcasting. We have found that people who don't understand podcasts are still often willing to watch a video on our websites. Many Flash video files do not look as good because they use a streaming file format with a lower frame rate and lower data rates.

Embedded Flash Players

A number of sites offer embedded Flash players; here are a two we've tried and like.

- **Podango** (www.podango. com). This hosting company makes all of their podcasts available with embedded players that offer both download and iTunes subscriptions.
- **Pyro TV** (www.pyro.tv). This is an online video-sharing site that can take your podcasting feed and repurpose it for web sharing. The service is free, but you have to submit your show for consideration since there are no costs involved to the podcaster.

Embedded Flash players are popular with web site browsers.

Adobe Media Player

The Adobe Media Player software is a newer option from Adobe and is built on Flash technology. The idea, though, was to create a platform that freed Flash video from requiring a live Internet connection and allowed offline viewing. Additionally, the Adobe Media Player has several options that focus on tracking and monetization.

The Adobe Media Player can also play back H.264 video.

Because the player supports both RSS and H.264 media, the opportunities for podcasters to utilize the technology are great. The player also makes it easier to monetize content via advertising and customization. It is built to address some of the complaints traditional broadcasters have had with podcasting in that it can provide anonymous measurement reports and copy protection.

YouTube

Now owned by Google, YouTube began in early 2005. It quickly rose to the top of video-sharing websites by offering user-generated and professionally created video content. The service uses both Flash and H.264 video as the underlying architecture. But it makes the whole process transparent to the end user through a relatively easy-to-use web interface. Additionally, YouTube has tie-ins with Apple and Adobe software, which offer direct publishing in their consumer lines of software.

While YouTube is very popular, many podcasters avoid it. The site has a fleamarket feel with its free-for-all approach. For example, a podcaster's content can get grouped with content that is off topic or with a direct competitor. YouTube also does not make it easy for podcasters to monetize their content through advertising. As such, YouTube views are often seen as taking away from a podcasts' financial opportunity. Many see YouTube as the antithesis of podcasting because you must go to the website and pull media down, whereas podcasting is built around a push model in which media is sent out.

Our take is to use YouTube as a promotional tool. Therefore, place some of your content online with them if your podcast has broad consumer appeal. For podcasts that target niche or professional markets, you may want to avoid the website altogether and instead harness the power of embedded Flash players that you promote and make available on your own.

Windows Media/Silverlight

While Windows Media and Silverlight are two very different technologies, they have several things in common. Microsoft makes them both, they both continue to evolve quickly, and they are both easier to create on a PC, but offer some Mac and Linux support.

Microsoft®
Silverlight™

Windows Media Player is the default media player for the Windows operating system. With that said, it does not tie in very well with Microsoft's own portable media player, the Zune. We don't recommend releasing podcasts as Windows Media files, because implementing MPEG-4 and H.264 on PCs is easy.

Microsoft Silverlight is a proprietary application that works with web browsers. It can be used to the provide animation, vector graphics, and video playback capabilities of Windows Presentation Foundation. Silverlight can also play back WMV, WMA, and MP3 media content, but it lacks support for traditional video podcasting formats. Silverlight requires much more knowledge about web programming than podcasting, and at this point is not a viable option for most podcasters. However, it's worth keeping an eye on, as Microsoft's technology continues to evolve with a mindset of reaching and serving the enterprise-level business market.

DVD Video

Many podcasters still harness the power of DVD as a distribution tool. After all, DVDs are easy to create and manufacture and can often be sold at a profit. Podcasters can put together favorite episodes or segments, and then make the compliation available for sale. Through websites like CreateSpace (www.createspace.com), you can create and sell DVDs using an on-demand model.

Of course, traditional manufacturing means are also available and can be more profitable. They just require that the podcaster be capable of carrying out inventory and fulfilling orders.

Regardless, keeping some DVDs of your content around is an easy way to share and distribute your shows with those less plugged in to podcasting.

Compression Tools

There are many video compression (or encoding) tools on the market. Knowing which one (or ones) to pick is a process of reading reviews as well as trial and error. Unfortunately, older tools such as Cleaner XL and Procoder have not kept up on newer formats like H.264. On the other hand, less expensive compression tools have emerged for the price-sensitive podcasting audience.

Essential Features

When selecting a tool for encoding video, we look at several aspects including speed, reliability, and price. These types of factors are somewhat subjective, and will vary based on the podcaster's budget, operating system, and specific needs. Here are a few features we look for when evaluating tools.

A good compression tool should offer broad support for presets, as well as the ability to filter and resize your video. Stomp from shinywhitebox.com is a powerful and affordable Mac tool.

- **MPEG-4 Support.** Support for the more basic MPEG-4 video using the "Simple Profile" is fairly common. With that said, make sure your encoding tool of choice supports this older format.

- **H.264 Support.** Make sure that the encoding tool can create podcast files using the modern part 10 protocols we discussed earlier. Older versions of encoding tools may not offer this, but the newer versions generally do.
- **Apple Compatible Presets.** You need a good starting point for your media compression settings. Look for a tool that offers podcasting or iPod presets.
- **Customized Presets.** An important feature is the ability to modify presets or create your own. By storing customized presets, you can ensure consistent results that are tailored to fit your podcast's needs.
- **Compression Preview.** Through a compression preview, you can simulate what the end file will look like before you invoke a compression pass. This is a useful way to visualize what changes to data rate and codec settings will mean for your audience.
- **Batch Processing.** The ability to batch process files is an essential time-saver. It allows you to add multiple files to the encoding tool, and then apply presets to the files. This essentially means that the time-intensive tasks of compression can be run as unsupervised jobs overnight or on weekends. This is an effective way to make money or at least save time as it allows you to focus on other tasks.

Affordable Compression Tools

Because podcasting technology has embraced consumers, there are many affordable (or even free) options to create podcast-ready video files. The biggest difference here is that many of these tools lack batch processing and offer minimal support for customized presets.

- **QuickTime Pro** (www.apple.com/quicktime/pro). This versatile tool makes it easy to convert video from one format to another. QuickTime Pro is a cross-platform solution that lets Mac and Windows users convert video files so they work with Apple's portable media players. The files that QuickTime produces are very compatible but don't offer as many options as other tools. QuickTime sells for $29.99 and is a preferred tool for most media pros' toolbox.
- **iTunes** (www.apple.com/itunes). While generally thought of as a podcasting client, iTunes can be used to convert incompatible media to an iPod/iPhone-ready format. Additionally, iTunes is essential for testing your files to see if they are compatible with Apple's portable media players. iTunes is a free, cross-platform solution.
- **iMovie/GarageBand** (www.apple.com/ilife). Apple offers a video editing and audio editing toolset as part of their iLife application suite. This software is bundled with all Mac

The Official Specs from Apple

If you want to know more about compression that follows the Apple protocols, visit www.apple.com/itunesstore/podcasttextspecs.html. This has every single technical spec on one page—compression advice, common mistakes, sample code, categories for podcasting, and so on. This is a good page to bookmark as well as to watch for changes.

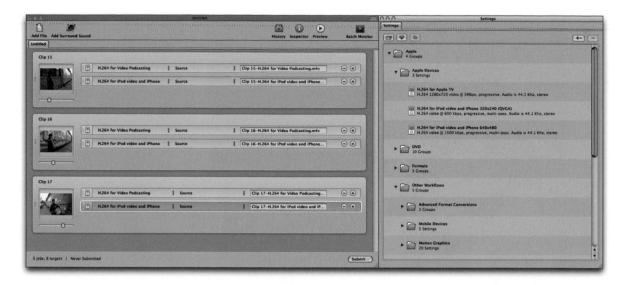

Apple's Compressor is bundled with Final Cut Studio. It offers a full-featured toolset and tight integration with Final Cut Pro.

speed. The product is only sold as part of the bundled Final Cut Studio suite, which means you likely have it already if you are using Final Cut Pro or Motion. Otherwise the suite is too comprehensive to buy just for this one application.

- **Sorenson Squeeze** (www.sorensonmedia.com). Sorenson offers several variations of their Squeeze product line depending on the features that you want. This is a cross-platform solution and is very popular due to its ease of use. The product's price varies depending on whether you need Flash Video support and which platform you choose to use. This is the leading PC product on the market. Sorenson also offers a hardware option for faster compression.

- **Telestream Episode and Episode Pro** (www.telestream.net). The Episode Series offers several options for encoding media to several formats. The tools are Mac only. They offer both customizable presets and a flexible filtering engine for improving video. The products are also very fast and have had frequent updates with improved features. The most common tools used by podcasters are the Episode and Episode Pro packages. These are desktop encoders that use the computer's hardware to perform the encode.

- **Adobe Media Encoder** (www.adobe.com). The Adobe Media Encoder is not a stand-alone product. Rather, it is a core technology in the Adobe Creative Suite products that work with video. You can easily access it through products like Premiere Pro. It supports several formats besides podcasting and offers excellent control.

Faster H.264 on a Mac

If you want to dramatically speed up the creation of H.264 files, be sure to take a look at Turbo.264 from Elgato (www.elgato.com). This accelerator plugs into a USB port and can decrease processing time by 400%. This is really a great way to quickly optimize clips with presets for iPods, Apple TV, and PSPs. Priced at $99, this is an easy way to save time when compressing podcasts.

Encoding Advice

There are four major facets that will shape your compression or encoding approach. We call them the "ilities" to make them easier to remember.

1. **Portability.** How easy is it to move the file from one device to another? Is the compressed file small enough to transfer via the Internet (and at what connection speed)?
2. **Compatibility.** Can multiple applications, hardware players, and web browsers view the file?
3. **Affordability.** Are the codec or hardware requirements within your budget? Are there any licensing fees involved?
4. **Quality.** Does the image or sound quality match your audience's needs?

If you keep these four aspects of podcasting files in mind, the following advice will make sense.

The Language of Compression Simplified

There are several bits of lingo that will pop up when you are working with compression software. Here are the most common ones with their plain English translations.

- **Architecture.** This is like the global family or classification of a file. It includes families such as MPEG, QuickTime, Windows Media, AIFF, etc. It is the "global" picture.
- **Batch Processing.** A benefit of many compression utilities is that they allow you to set up several files to run at once, so you can walk away and leave your computer working hard.
- **Bit Rate.** How much data per second is there in your file? The higher the number, the larger the file.
- **Channels.** Most common will be the choice between stereo and mono. Stereo files use two channels of audio data and occupy twice the space as mono files.
- **Codec.** Stands for compressor/decompressor. The algorithm of code allows for further shrinking of the files. In some cases, compressors cost additional money to the content creator. Decompressors are usually free to improve the distribution plan and market share.
- **Compress.** The process of shrinking the file using mathematical algorithms. Modern compression techniques are significantly more effective than their historical counterparts.
- **Pixel Aspect Ratio.** Computer pixels are square; digital video pixels can be rectangular or non-square. The video editing software or playback device (such as a television) usually compensates for this. Since you plan to show the video on a computer or an iPod, you will need to manually resize the document to the right shape.
- **Resolution.** Also called sample size, resolution is the number of bits used by the computer to describe the analog data. Audio CDs are usually 16-bit. Bigger resolution gives higher quality.
- **Sampling Rate.** The number of samples captured per second. Audio CDs are usually 44.1 kHz while digital video is usually 48 kHz. Bigger sampling rate gives higher quality.
- **Variable Bit Rate (VBR) Compression.** One of the most effective ways to create smaller files. The computer analyzes the video file before compressing the data. Encoding this way is far slower, but if you can, choose this method for superior results.

Simple Techniques for Better Compression

There are a lot of easy things you can do to make your podcasts look better. These things usually happen in the compression software via filters and image processing. The more of these you can fix, the better the results you'll get. Every compression tool is different, but you'll usually find these options in the export dialog box or help menus.

Start Big … Finish Small

Be sure to work with original source material or low compressed sources. By sticking with DV or better quality, you'll get better compression and smaller file sizes. Recompressing a previously compressed file produces additional artifacts (imagine making a photocopy of a photocopy).

De-interlace Your Video

Most NTSC and PAL video files are interlaced; some HD videos are also interlaced. This means that half of one image is blended with half of the next. On a television, this produces smoother motion; on a computer or portable media player, it produces junk.

Most compression software offers a de-interlace option via a checkbox or filter. If you are shrinking the video down to the smaller 320 × 240 size, the basic de-interlace filter is fine to use. If you are targeting a 640 × 480 size video, then be sure to use an

The video frame on the left shows interlacing in the fast-moving areas. The frame on the right shows the interlacing removed.

advance de-interlace option (such as blend or interpolate). These generate better quality, but can add significant processing time.

Lower Your Audio Standards

You can often lower the audio quality of your podcasting files. Digital video generally uses a sample rate of 48 kHz, while audio CDs use 44.1 kHz. The audio is also usually delivered in 16-bit. If your audio is not complex (such as voice only) you can cut your sample rate. Different tools allow you to change to different rates depending on codec. You can try a sample rate of 44.1, 32, 22, or 11 kHz and a sample size of 8-bit. This can produce unnoticeable audio changes, but save space.

Shrink the Window

You don't need to make video postage stamp sized. But reducing the window to half size creates a file that is 25% the file size of the original. That's a BIG savings in space. A 640 × 480 window is also much smaller than an HD podcast. Strongly evaluate the size that you use to deliver your video podcast.

Reshape the Video

Most likely you are working with a video file that is 720 × 480 or 720 × 576 pixels. You need to resize this to 640 × 480 for it to properly display on the computer monitor or podcast screen (640 × 360 if wide-screen video). You must compensate for pixel aspect ratio with your podcasts. Additionally, you cannot exceed a width of 640 or a height of 480 if you want the files to work on a portable media player.

Going to Flash as Well?

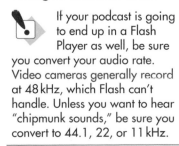

If your podcast is going to end up in a Flash Player as well, be sure you convert your audio rate. Video cameras generally record at 48 kHz, which Flash can't handle. Unless you want to hear "chipmunk sounds," be sure you convert to 44.1, 22, or 11 kHz.

Be sure that your video is being sized to no wider than 640 pixels for use on a portable media player. The correct width is 640 × 480 for 4:3 video and 640 × 360 for 16:9 video. For half-screen video, divide these numbers in half. Like most pro-level compression tools, the Adobe Media Encoder gives you precise control over size and reshaping.

The Rule of 8

Be sure that any dimension you use for a codec is divisible by 8. When a dimension can be divided by 8, it allows the codec to work most efficiently. Otherwise the codec must do additional processing before displaying the material. This results in longer encode times as well as increased challenges for the playback machine.

Restore the Washed-out Picture

Video signals usually operate between RGB values of 16 through 235. On the other hand, computers use an RGB value of 0 through 255. You will need to restore the black and white points of your image. Many applications have this option built in as a filter.

The biggest concern is to restore (or crush) the blacks. This will help reduce visible noise in the file and result in a cleaner compression. Look for options called "Black–White Restore" or something similar. Usually the default preset will work. You can always adjust the filter until unwanted noise is removed in the shadowy areas. This is essential if your material contains shadowy or dark areas.

Improve the Saturation

A video file intended for podcast may also need the saturation turned up a bit. This is to compensate for what we call the "Wal-Mart effect." Consumer TVs have their reds over-cranked to make skin tones appear richer on their cheap tubes. As such, consumers

are used to viewing rich reds and saturated images. Just be careful to not overdue it, or your talent will look like they fell asleep in a tanning bed. Many compression tools lack a saturation effect, so be sure to boost the saturation within your NLE if needed.

Frame Rate Reduction

Fortunately, the MPEG-4 compression is very good and space saving. However, you can still often see a benefit in file size by reducing frame rate. One method involves shooting the video at 24 fps, which results in less material to encode. Another technique is to cut the frame rate in half after you've shot (such as dropping to 15 fps for NTSC or 12 fps for PAL). These tests are worth trying in your experimentation to determine the right settings for your video.

Test Your Settings

Your quest for "perfect" compression will involve trial and error (often a lot of trial and a little too much error). A good place to start will be the default podcasting settings your compression tool offers. Duplicate this setting, and rename it (such as Podcast_Large_2). Then modify a few of the variables we've discussed here. Remember, the biggest impact will be the data rate of your podcast (and don't exceed the upper limits discussed earlier). You will often make several settings that are only slightly different, then test them.

There's More to Life Than iTunes

You need to remember that there are other podcast aggregators on the market, and you should test your files and podcast feeds using them. Here are three popular options:

- **Sony Media Manager PRO for PSP** (www.sonycreativesoftware.com)
- **Zune Marketplace** (www.zune.net)
- **Miro** (www.getmiro.com)
- **ZENcast Organizer** (www.zencast.com)

Looking for a Great Source on Web Compression

 One of the resources I find most useful for current information on web compression is www.proappstips.com. Here you'll find a wonderful PDF available called *Simple Encoding Recipes for the Web*. These recipes are just that, step-by-step directions for popular tools such as Compressor, Squeeze, and Episode. The information works well for podcasting and covers other delivery methods such as YouTube and web pages as well. The PDF sells for $4.95, and its author Philip Hodgetts is a respected member of the professional video community. This is a highly recommended resource of ours. It even includes links to web pages, so you can compare the results side by side.

Before you compress a lot of video, create a small test file. Try compressing 30 seconds of video with different settings. This test file should ideally include a mixture of the footage and graphics that will be in your finished shows. The goal is to find compression settings that work well with your material and that are compatible with the technology your audience wants to use.

Always (and we mean *always*) test each setting by taking its files and transferring them to an intended player. Put the file on an iPod and an iPhone, put it on a PSP, put it on a laptop, look at it on a Mac and Windows box, or try a Microsoft Zune. You need to test your settings because something can go wrong with the file. Trust us, we've been burned; we've had podcasts with five-star ratings drop to a three-star rating because reviewers complained about files not working. So you have to be very careful if your podcast is being ranked or rated. Post bad files and the backlash can be very strong. If it's any incentive, you may be able to write off the cost of additional technology on your taxes (discuss with your accountant).

PRO*file*: CreativeCOW.net After Effects Podcast

The CreativeCOW.net After Effects Tutorials Podcast is a weekly video training podcast with tutorials covering tips and techniques for viewers who want to get the most out of Adobe After Effects. Since its first episode in December of 2005, it has proven to be the world's most popular After Effects podcast and has stayed in iTunes top 20 for Software How-To's.

Photo ©Chris Macke

Rabinowitz got into podcasting at the suggestion of others: "I had made a few video tutorials for CreativeCOW.net, and the COW team asked if I would be willing to convert those tutorials for a new podcast they wanted to start. Honestly, at the time I knew almost nothing about podcasting, and from what I did know, I thought it was just a fad," says Rabinowitz. "Since the real work was already done, I figured I didn't have anything to lose, so I went for it."

The show is hosted and produced by Aharon Rabinowitz, who is creative director at All Bets Are Off Productions (www.allbetsareoff.com), a New York City-based company specializing in video, animation, and dynamic media. In addition, Aharon teaches advanced animation classes at Pratt Manhattan and trains animation professionals in and around NYC.

The CreativeCOW.net After Effects podcast falls into the genre called screen-casting. This is where the host creates a tutorial about a software application, and viewers can see what the host is doing on their computer screen.

Rabinowitz has done an excellent job connecting with his audience. His personalized style and subject matter expertise quickly drew a loyal following.

"Within a few episodes, based on subscription and emails, it became clear that podcasting was a powerful tool for reaching a large audience. People were really into it, and they let us know it."

The two tools that Rabinowitz uses most are Techsmith's Camtasia, to record his screen demos, and a microphone. He highly recommends Plantronics mics for anyone who wants to produce screencasts.

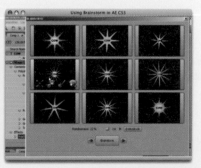

"If I had to choose one item that I can't live without, it would be my Plantronics DSP-500 headset. It delivers great quality audio at a comparatively cheap price ($50). They don't make them anymore, but they sell plenty of them on eBay."

Rabinowitz has learned several things in his time as a podcaster. He cautions podcasters to balance the data rate of their shows and thoroughly test their compression settings.

"Originally, when I compressed my video I was using larger data rates to keep the quality up—but that meant larger files that could take a long time to download, depending on where you were in the world. With the right compression tools—such as Sorenson Squeeze—you can keep the quality up while lowering the file size dramatically."

Rabinowitz also shared how he stays relevant to his audience. He emphasized paying attention to viewer comments and emails when generating new show ideas. He also tries to keep the viewer in mind when scripting his content.

"People like to be entertained, even when they are being educated. Don't be afraid to plan ahead—especially with jokes. If people have a good time listening/watching you, they'll come back for more. If you don't enjoy yourself in the process, then no one watching your show will either."

Entering the world of podcasting has opened up new professional opportunities for Rabinowitz. While he previously kept busy as an animator, he now has new clients calling.

"Podcasting has changed the course of my career. My interest in podcasting has allowed me to expand into the area of producing video for the web— There's no question that this area of technology is the next stage in the evolution of broadcasting and communication," says Rabinowitz. "More and more, my clients want to create content for the web, and, with the experience I've gained, I've been able to help them reach a significantly larger audience through that venue."

Gear List

- Techsmith Camtasia Studio
- Plantronics DSP 500 Headset/Mic
- Samson C03U multi-pattern USB studio condenser microphone
- BOLData desktop PC
- Adobe Production Studio
- Sorenson Squeeze compression suite
- Sony Cybershot camera (for taking pictures and movies used as source material in tutorials)

We recommend checking out Aharon Rabinowitz's latest work, "Internet Killed the Video Star: A Guide to Creating Video for the Web," which covers video compression, flash video, podcasting, and a workflow for creating tutorials.

9

HOSTING THE PODCAST

You've developed great content, executed a (near) flawless production, edited a masterpiece, and compressed it to a small file that works on an iPod … now what? Well, your podcast is ready to share with the world … so get it out there.

You'll need to place your podcast files on a file server that can be accessed from the Internet. You'll need to find a location that can handle the demands of large files and lots of requests. After all, podcasts are relatively large compared to typical files that are accessed with web browsers.

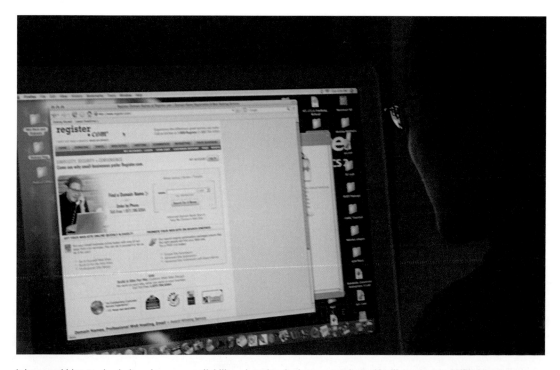

It is a good idea to check domain name availability when developing your podcast. You'll want a good URL to support your show.

The Essential Steps to Publish a Podcast

In this and our next chapter, we'll explore the steps needed to successfully publish a podcast for consumption by the masses. The process essentially involves four steps:

1. **Select or register your web address or domain name.** While you don't have to choose a URL for your podcast, it is a good idea to have a domain name associated with your show. Ultimately your audience will want to interact; giving them a website to visit is essential to building an audience and a brand. You can use an existing website to host a blog and your podcast feed or you can register a new domain name. Popular registration services include **www. Register.com** and **www.GoDaddy.com**.

2. **Select a podcast-hosting option.** You need to find a storage solution that matches your hosting needs. This will be a combination of total storage and bandwidth allowances as well as technical support and customer service.

3. **Build a blog.** Adding a blog to a podcast is essential if you want to build an audience. Your viewers can interact in forums, download resources related to your shows, and find additional opportunities to learn. A blog will also

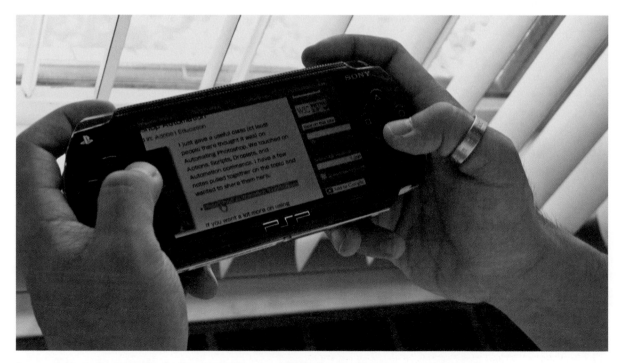

Some portable media players like the iPod Touch, iPhone, and PlayStation Portable can browse your blog.

give you a chance to monetize your viewership by offering products for sale. We'll address blogging solutions in our next chapter.

4. **Create an RSS feed.** This is how your audience can subscribe to the content. A valid RSS feed is required for your podcast to be listed in directories. We'll explore RSS feed creation in our next chapter.

Budgeting for Hosting

We generally equate serving video on the Internet to hiring a caterer to serve a party. If you buy too much, it's just wasteful and you'll have leftovers that won't keep (after all, you pay for bandwidth whether you use it or not). On the other hand, if you're too conservative and don't get enough, everyone stands around complaining and no one goes away satisfied.

Therefore, it's critical that you attempt to estimate and then measure your audience. What you are trying to do is estimate how much storage and bandwidth you need. Try to determine how many people are going to pull down each episode … initially this may be a guess, but an attempt at accuracy is better than none at all. Additionally, how many episodes do you want to have up at a time? You have to weigh the total usage (or bandwidth) you need as well as how much total storage you want.

Unlimited Bandwidth

There are dedicated podcast-hosting servers that are different than web-hosting services. These generally have very low prices. You want a plan that has a no-bandwidth charge, so if your podcast viewership goes through the roof, you're not paying through the nose for it. The last thing you want is a podcast that costs you a bunch of money to make and then a bunch more money just to deliver (especially if you're not making direct money off the show).

Finding a Good Domain Name

You'll likely want to find a custom URL that matches the name or content of your podcast. This will give you a website property that you can develop to support your show. The dot-com names are the most popular, but you can choose others such as dot-tv, dot-net, or dot-org depending on the content of your show. The domain registration services have search engines for finding available names. Here are a few practical pieces of advice when creating your custom URL:

- Try to find a URL that is short and easy to remember.
- Try to match your podcast name and URL if possible. This will create synergy and make it easier for your viewers to remember it.
- If you want your website to appear higher in search engine results, work the topic into the URL. For example, the URL www.PhotoshopforVideo.com ranks high when people search for information about Photoshop and video editing as well as for Photoshop training videos.
- Be sure to rent your domain for multiple years or set it to automatically renew. You don't want to build up a popular show and domain, then lose it because you forget to register it again.

Be sure to review the several different hosting plans available. Each offers different pricing structures and benefits

Free Hosting

There are several services that offer free podcast hosting. These plans generally offer a smaller amount of storage and may have bandwidth caps. These plans generally require you to use web-based tools for generating your RSS file. The biggest drawback is that most of these free plans will insert ads into your podcast (and they do not share revenue). With the large amount of afford-able hosting plans, we recommend staying away from "free" plans—after all, you get what you pay for.

The Costs of Using a Website-Hosting Service

There are several different providers of affordable website-hosting plans. These are *not* podcast-hosting plans. While the web plans may offer high bandwidth options, you may be in violation of the plan's agreement if you place large media files online.

When each media file is 20 to 80 MB, it is so easy to go over your bandwidth limit. We had a web-hosting plan with 20 TB of data transfer. We thought, "We'll never use that." We were wrong. We logged in a week and a half later and we had already incurred $100 in overage charges because iTunes had decided to put our podcast on the front page that week and everybody found it.

Even if you can afford the bandwidth, many web-hosting plans specifically identify large media files in their terms-of-service agreements. We have had entire websites suspended due to large files and high usage. Be sure to look closely at web-hosting agreements if you decide to go this route.

The short lesson here is choose a podcast-hosting plan with an unlimited bandwidth option.

One site offering free hosting is Podango. Not all podcasters are accepted, though. Podango offers free hosting and an advertising revenue-sharing model to podcasts that fit their model.

Affordable Hosting

The costs for podcast hosting vary greatly and will require the podcaster to evaluate each purchase based on several factors (which we'll explore in a moment). There are several moderately priced ($10–$50) plans that offer unlimited bandwidth and storage from 200 MB to a few GB. Most of these give you precise control over your RSS feed and allow a high level of customization. There are several "small" differences between plans, such as FTP access and detailed statistics. For podcasters with high volume needs, several hosting companies offer larger plans.

Self-Hosting

If your company runs its own server, you can certainly consider hosting your podcast files yourself. We just highly recommend having a discussion with the IT department early on. Some of our clients who chose to add dedicated servers for podcasts, but most have been content with an enterprise-level hosting plan from an outside provider, keeping their RSS feed on their own servers. We'll explore this option in this and the next chapter.

Offsite, Dedicated Hosting

Many web-hosting companies offer dedicated servers that you can use for your podcast. If you are willing to pay for the entire machine, they'll provide the service and Internet connection. For example, GoDaddy offers 600 GB of storage and 2000 GB of transfer per month for about $250. Depending on how big your show gets, be sure to consider using a dedicated host. You should also weigh the costs of renting a server versus installing and maintaining your own (and the required network connection). We often find that external solutions are best unless the client has a long history of running their own servers at very high bandwidths.

Hosting Requirements

Podcasters have some unique requirements when it comes time to finding the right home for their video files. It's important that your hosting company support the workflow you desire. Do you plan to upload files with an FTP program? Do you want to host your RSS feed on your own website? Do you want the hosting company to generate your RSS feed for you? There are several questions to ask when looking for the right host.

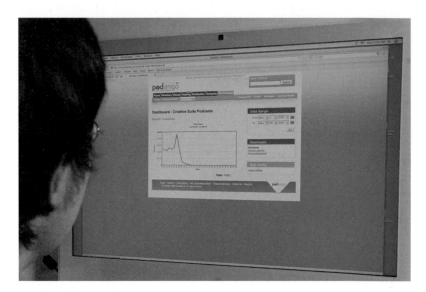

Be sure to track your bandwidth usage over time. It's important to keep an eye on it, or you may get expensive overage charges or have your site shut down.

Bandwidth

Podcast files can get relatively big ... combine that with even a relatively moderately sized audience and you need a lot of bandwidth. The term *bandwidth* is used to describe the amount of data that can be transferred as part of the chosen hosting plan. An easy way to think of this is as the monthly data transfer rate.

Exceeding your bandwidth limits generally has two outcomes. The first is that your files can be "capped," which means that your show (and possibly website) will no longer download. This is an undesirable outcome, as your site will appear to essentially stop working. The other likely scenario is overage charges. Just like what happens when you go over your allotted minutes on a cell phone plan, overage charges can add up very quickly.

Storage

Depending on the type of podcast-hosting plan you choose, your amount of total storage will vary. Just how much storage do you need? Well it really depends on how many episodes you want to have online at once. Do you want to keep all of your episodes available in an archive? Will you just keep the current episode up? The answer probably falls somewhere in between.

Take a look at the average size of your video podcast files. Then multiply that size by the number of episodes you'd like to keep online at once. For example, if your average episode size is 40 MB and you want to keep 20 episodes up at once, you'll need about 800 MB. In order to allow for flexibility, you should choose a 1 GB hosting plan in this scenario.

RSS Tools

Several podcast-hosting plans offer a suite of RSS tools. Many of the sites are designed to offer web-based feed generation tools.

How Much Is Enough?

Determining how much storage and bandwidth you need can be a bit tricky when you try to think in abstracts. So let's take a sample scenario. When we release a 5-minute podcast in our Photoshop for Video series, it's about 20 MB. If we release four of these in a month, we need 80 MB of storage. If our audience of 500 downloads each episode in a month, we'd need about 40 GB of bandwidth. Notice how quickly video podcasts consume bandwidth? In fact, we have *far* more than 500 viewers … and we consume *a lot* of bandwidth. As such, the unlimited bandwidth plans are the only way to go as soon as your audience grows.

Disputed Statistics

Many tracking services "discount" their numbers to try and filter out "false hits." You might experience underreporting if your episodes are going into places like colleges and universities, since these environments can be using distributed IP addresses. Try to focus less on the hard numbers and more on the trends for your show. Look at change over time and see what is happening to your podcast.

You can create the RSS feed by simply filling information into a web form. We'll explore the option to create web-generated RSS feeds in our next chapter. These RSS tools are good for the podcaster who does not want to have to learn another skill (such as writing RSS code).

Statistics

In order for your podcast to grow, it's important that you both target and track niche markets. If you want advertisers, then statistics are essential. If you need to prove the "effectiveness" or "reach" of your podcast, you'll also need numbers. In fact, we're big proponents of measurement, so you can learn from both your successes and failures. Without measurement, your shows are operating in a vacuum.

You can get very accurate statistics about downloads. Through services like Podtrac, you can get statistics on a per-country basis. You can quickly learn where your podcast is being consumed

Services like Podtrac help you better understand your audience.

Third-Party Statistics with Podtrac

You can get your own statistics for free thanks to Podtrac (www.Podtrac.com). Their service is designed to help podcasters measure their audiences through both tracking and audience surveys. The system essentially works by giving each podcast episode a unique code that is entered into the RSS feed. Then, with each download, the files are counted.

Additionally, Podtrac has a matching service and brokers ads, as well as offers information you can use on your own to line up ads. The tracking service is free, but Podtrac will take a portion of any ad sales they line up for your show. The Podtrac numbers are acceptable to most advertisers as an accurate way to track viewership.

and on what computer platform. Additionally, you can see when a show is downloaded and how consumers react to show topics. In this way, you can learn from your strengths and your weaknesses, and evaluate how individual episodes are doing.

Upload via File Transfer Protocol

The use of File Transfer Protocol (FTP) is a convenient way to transfer multiple files to a server. The convenience is that you can transfer multiple files simultaneously (which lets you set up a large transfer, then walk away from the working computer). Additionally, an interrupted file transfer can often be resumed. Virtually all computer platforms support FTP protocol, but not all server-hosting companies enable FTP access as part of their podcast-hosting plans.

If you plan on having several shows to upload at once, then look for a host that offers FTP access. This can be a big time saver, as it allows you direct access to your files on the server (as opposed to using a slower web interface). FTP access is less common in hosting plans, because it requires hosting companies to open up their servers directly. While security protocols are easy to implement, many service providers don't offer this option. Be sure to check if FTP access is an option for hosting companies you are considering.

Upload via Browser

The alternative to FTP access is using a web browser to load the files. This style of hosting services generally requires you to enter the details for the podcast episode via a web browser, then click a button to select a file on your local hard drive in order to transfer the file.

While this style of hosting is simple, it doesn't offer the flexibility of FTP access. We recommend browser-based solutions for clients with low-volume podcast needs (that is to say, only a few episodes to load each week). It is possible to find a host that offers both browser and FTP solutions, which gives you the flexibility to choose a solution based on your personal comfort level and needs.

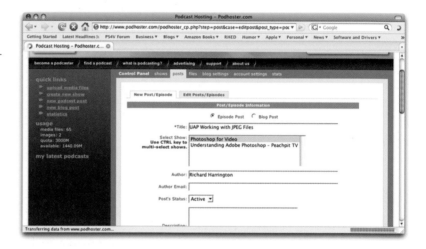

Advertising Model

Many podcast-hosting services defer their costs through the use of ads. The less you pay for podcast hosting, the more likely there will be ads on your shows or on the show's web page. There are other services that attempt to sell ads for you and then keep a percentage of those sales.

Regardless of the host's policy toward ads, you will need to determine your show's own rules. Some podcasts need to run advertising-free because the client or sponsor wants the show to appear unbiased. Other shows are simply looking to cover their costs. Be sure to investigate your options when considering the financial prospects of your podcast.

Use of Private Domain

Many hosting solutions are self-contained, which is to say your media files and RSS feed must stay on the hosting company's servers. While this is desirable for media files (after all, you want the bandwidth and support of the hosting company), it is less so for RSS files. Many podcasters (and clients) want the RSS file to live on their own website. Ask yourself what's more desirable, www.yourdomain.com/podcast.xml or yourdomain.podcasthostingcompany.com.

Looking for More Hosting Options?

There's a useful chart available to browse several popular podcast-hosting solutions. Just visit www.okaytoplay.com/wiki/Podcast_Hosting.

Keeping control over where your RSS feed lives is an important detail.

In general, the best option is to keep the RSS feed on your own website. This way, browsing customers can choose to explore the rest of your site after they've looked at your RSS feed. If having your own private domain is not an option, look for a host that lets you put together a customized landing page on your own website. The more customized you can make this page, the better. We'll explore options for displaying your RSS feed in our next chapter.

Hosting Options

There are several podcast-hosting companies in the market. Each offers a unique mix of services, technical options, and pricing. In our own experience, we have worked with three different hosting providers and continue to do so. The right host means balancing the factors we've discussed in this chapter with the needs of your show or client.

Here are a few popular solutions well suited to video podcast hosting. Be sure to look at their individual websites, as pricing and technical details will likely change with time.

In iTunes Doesn't Mean *On* iTunes

A common misperception is that having your show listed in the iTunes directory means that your files are on Apple's servers. This is just not the case. The iTunes directory is just that, a directory. It helps consumers find podcasts in an organized fashion. Submitting your show to the iTunes Store for inclusion simply gets your show listed. You are still responsible for finding your own hosting service.

Hosting Service	Cost per Month	Bandwidth	Storage
AltarCast (www.altarcast.com)	$29–249	Unlimited	Unlimited
Apple .Mac (www.apple.com/dotmac)	$8.33	100 GB	10 GB
AvMyPodcast (www.avmypodcast.com)	$4.95–24.95	Unlimited	250 MB to 2 GB
Big Contact (v2.bigcontact.com)	Free	Unlimited	Unlimited
CacheFly (www.blogamp.com)	$15–299	30–1200 GB	300 MB to 2 GB
GoDaddy Quick Podcast (www.godaddy.com)	$4.24–19.99	100–500 GB	1–10 GB
Hipcast (www.hipcast.com)	$4.95–49.95	5 GB to Unlimited	5 MB to 5 GB
Libsyn (www.libsyn.com)	$5–30	Unlimited	100–800 MB
Libsyn Pro (www.libsynpro.com)	Negotiated	Unlimited	Negotiated
MyPodcasts.net (www.mypodcasts.net)	$9.95–19.95	Unlimited	500 MB to 2 GB
Ourmedia (www.ourmedia.org)	Free	Unlimited	Unlimited
Podango (www.podango.com)	Free or custom	Unlimited	Negotiated
Podbean (www.podbean.com)	Free to $39.95	Unlimited	100 MB to 4 GB
podblaze (www.podblaze.com)	$14–97	2–20 GB	200 MB to 1 GB
podbus (www.podbus.com)	$5	200 GB	10 GB
Podcast FM (www.podcastfm.co.uk)	Free to £39.95	Unlimited	30 MB to Unlimited
Podcast Spot (www.podcastspot.com)	Free to $56	Unlimited	Unlimited
Podhoster.com (www.podhoster.com)	$4.95–29.95	Unlimited	250 MB to 2 GB
Podkive (www.genetichosting.com)	$10–375	Unlimited	100 MB to 120 GB
PodStrike!™ Podcast Manager (www.podstrike.com)	Free to $19.95	Unlimited	50 MB to 10 GB
switchpod (www.switchpod.com)	Free to $30	Unlimited	200 MB to 5 GB
WildVoice (www.wildvoice.com)	Free	Unlimited	200 MB to 2 GB

RSS Tools	Statistics	FTP Upload	Browser Upload	Advertising	Private Domain
Yes	No	Yes	Yes	Yes	No
Yes	No	Yes	Yes	No	Yes
Yes	No	No	Yes	Yes	No
Yes	Yes	Yes	No	Yes	Yes
No	Yes	Yes	Yes	Yes	No
Yes	Yes	No	Yes	Yes	Yes
Yes	No	No	Yes	Yes	Yes
Yes	Yes	Yes	Yes	Yes	Yes
Yes	Yes	Yes	Yes	Yes	Yes
Yes	Yes	Yes	Yes	Yes	No
Yes	No	Yes	Yes	Yes	No
Yes	Yes	Yes	Yes	Yes	Yes
Yes	No	No	Yes	Yes	No
Yes	Yes	No	Yes	Yes	No
Yes	No	Yes	Yes	Yes	No
Yes	Yes	Yes	Yes	Yes	No
Yes	Yes	No	Yes	Yes	Yes
Yes	No	Yes	Yes	Yes	No
Yes	Yes	Yes	Yes	Yes	Yes
Yes	Yes	Yes	Yes	Yes	Yes
Yes	Yes	Yes	Yes	Yes	No
Yes	Yes	No	Yes	Yes	No

10

CREATING THE FEED

Without a properly formatted RSS feed, your podcast is a great idea that's stuck on a media server. This is because the podcast directories and podcast aggregators require a valid feed so the media can be indexed, browsed, and subscribed to.

The podcast uses an RSS feed, which is similar to the technology behind several popular news websites. Next time you visit a website and see a small orange icon on the right edge of the address bar, click it to view the RSS feed directly. What you'll discover is that a modern web browser can quickly sift and sort the information on the page.

A valid XML feed is easier to read if you load it into a program optimized for coding such as BBEdit, TextMate, or SubEthaEdit.

The XML file associated with your page allows for really simple syndication (hence the name, RSS) and it allows these text entries to be easily syndicated, or in other words, packaged, distributed, and consumed. The end user can collect the page's content without actually having to revisit the web page. As soon as something new is added to the page, the RSS reader or web browser indicates that new content is ready.

An Overview of RSS

RSS technology was designed with convenience as the primary goal. The purpose of RSS is to make it easier for your audience to find out about new content and have that information delivered to their computer. Because people are interested in many topics, RSS makes it easier to keep up on the latest information (without much effort).

RSS is an XML-based form of code. It allows the structured publishing of lists of hyperlinks, along with other descriptive information (or metadata). This information lets viewers decide which content they want to view or receive. A simple bit of software, known as the feed reader or feed catcher, checks regularly to see if the RSS feed contains new information. People can set their computer to fetch this information and display it. A common use is headline tickers or sidebars that people enable on their computer. For example, Windows Vista users can subscribe to RSS feeds and have the information appear above their desktop in a floating box. This makes it easy to see the news a viewer is most interested in.

A Brief History of RSS

The RSS formats evolved from several earlier attempts at syndication. The ideas grew from the concept of restructuring the information found on websites. This work is thought to have begun by Ramanathan V. Guha and others in Apple Computer's Advanced Technology Group in 1995. This then evolved into the Resource Description Framework (RDF) site summary, the first version of RSS. RDF was an XML standard devoted to describing information resources. This version became known as RSS 0.9 and was intended for use in the my.Netscape.com portal.

The technology continued to evolve, and in July of 1999 Dan Libby of Netscape produced a new version, called RSS 0.91. This version was further simplified and incorporated elements of Dave Winer's Scripting News syndication format. The technology was renamed Rich Site Summary (RSS). The technology had several early adopters because many web publishers wanted to make their content compatible with the dominant Netscape Navigator web browser. Support for RSS waned, though, as new Netscape owner America Online dropped support and all documentation and tools from the Netscape site.

Two different development parties emerged to take up the RSS mantle and continue development (without the approval of NetscapeThe RSS-DEV Working Group and Dave Winer competed to create tools and refine the RSS technology, producing different versions of RSS.

In December 2000, Winer released RSS 0.92, which offered the enclosure element. The enclosure element allowed for the addition of audio and video files (and hence served as a spark for podcasting). In September 2002, Winer released a major new version of RSS. Appropriately named RSS 2.0, the format was re-dubbed "Really Simple Syndication."

The copyright for RSS was assigned to Harvard's Berkman Center for the Internet & Society in July 2003. At the same time the RSS Advisory Board was launched to maintain and publish the specifications. The group is also charged with addressing questions and developing a community for RSS. The group continues to evolve the specification and address ambiguities in the technology that better enable web developers to deliver content.

The RSS Icon

The RSS icon first appeared in the Mozilla Firefox web browser. Microsoft then adopted it for use in Internet Explorer and Outlook. The Opera web browser then followed along. This made the orange square with white radio waves the industry standard. Notably, Apple's Safari browser does not follow suit.

What Can RSS Do?

The true beauty of RSS lies in its flexibility. A single RSS feed can be read by a multitude of hardware and software technologies. Consumers like RSS because it cuts down on them having to remember to go to their favorite websites. In 2005, Apple introduced video-capable iPods and enabled support for video podcasting in iTunes (mainly as a way to fill the iPod with free content). TiVo has gotten on board with the ability to either read podcasts from a computer in your house or directly subscribe to podcasts via RSS. TiVo offers channels with preloaded, select podcasts, and you can manually (and painfully) enter an RSS address with the remote control. Other consumer devices, like Apple TV, Microsoft Zune and X-Box, and Sony PSP and PlayStation 3, have also gotten on board. Cell phone manufacturers are starting to add the ability to subscribe to podcasts on their mobile handhelds. Even many television manufacturers are building Internet-ready TVs with integrated RSS readers.

Despite the widespread support for portable and consumer electronics, don't lose sight of the fact that RSS is also supported by every major web browser, even Internet Explorer 7.0, which has been notoriously late to adopt accepted standards. An RSS feed can be easily "skinned" with Extensible Stylesheet Language Transformations (XSLT) by a web programmer or integrated into a site. This allows web developers to create a human-readable version of the XML powering the feed and integrate the constantly updating feed, yet still match the overall look of the site without any new programming. This is primarily done by the use

RSS and Podcasting

The evolution of podcasting is closely tied to RSS. Once a RSS feed is enabled, computers can fetch the content. You'll recall that an aggregator program, which pulls all of the feeds into a single interface, generally performs this task. The extension of the RSS 2.* branch allowed enclosures. This format has been widely adopted and is the current standard for podcasting (due largely in part to Apple adopting it for their iTunes software).

The Latest Thing?

When your clients say, "I want one of those new-fangled podcasts" you say, "Well, keep in mind that, while the term is a little new, it was invented in 2004, so it's not that new. It's just really a confluence or an evolution of a bunch of technologies that are now working together."

A valid RSS feed contains lots of useful information. Additionally, it can be subscribed to using several different computer and hardware devices.

of dynamic coding languages such as PHP or JavaScript, in conjunction with Cascading Style Sheets (CSS), which allows parameters like fonts and colors to be defined for display in a browser. While you'll likely need to explain RSS to your clients, you'll find that its integration and development is relatively simple compared to other web technologies.

Developing the Feed

The goal with podcasting is not only to have a feed that is technically compliant, but to have one that is well-written and that actually motivates casual browsers to come and view your content. As such, the feed must contain elements that help others find the show through web searches and enables the content to stand out when people browse podcast directories.

Writing the Copy

A podcast feed contains both creative writing and code. While you can choose to generate the code portion by hand or by using RSS feed software, you are on your own for the marketing copy. An RSS feed has several components that help define what a podcast is about. Let's take a look at the major elements that involve creative writing.

© istockphoto

- **Podcast Title.** Your show needs an effective title that connects with your audience. While there are lots of differing opinions about what makes a title good, we believe in simplicity and brevity. Keeping a name simple means avoiding unnecessary humor or wit that might be misunderstood by outsiders. Brevity means working the key topic early in the title, especially since many podcast search engines truncate titles when browsing.
- **Author.** You may think that this is an easy one, but it's not. You need to decide who should receive author credit for the show. Is this the name of your talent? Is it the sponsor? The production company? This is a tricky decision to make, and it should come down to which name carries the most weight. We generally favor the name of the primary host and the production company. This way casual searchers can find a show based on the "celebrity," and the production company also gains name recognition. Be prepared for the sponsor also wanting author credit; we usually recommend working the sponsor's name into the show's description instead.
- **Category.** You need to determine which categories your show appears in. You can specify up to three categories for your show for the text search view. For the image-based browse system and for placement in the Top Podcasts lists, only the first category is used. If you pick a subcategory, you'll automatically appear in the parent category. For example, a "Fashion & Beauty" listing in the iTunes Store would appear in the "Arts" category as well. Do not pick three categories just to have three. Make sure your podcast genuinely belongs in the categories you assign it. Miscategorized shows are often rejected from the iTunes Store as well as other directories.

iTunes Categories for Podcasting

The iTunes store uses several categories and subcategories to make the store easy to browse. Think of these as sections of a large bookstore, where books are grouped by topic to make the store easier to explore. While these categories are for the iTunes Store, many other websites have adopted them as well.

- Arts
  - Design
  - Fashion & Beauty
  - Food
  - Literature
  - Performing Arts
  - Visual Arts
- Business
  - Business News
  - Careers
  - Investing
  - Management & Marketing
  - Shopping
- Comedy
- Education
  - Education Technology
  - Higher Education
  - K-12
  - Language Courses
  - Training
- Games & Hobbies
  - Automotive
  - Aviation
  - Hobbies
  - Other Games
  - Video Games
- Government & Organizations
  - Local
  - National
  - Non-Profit
  - Regional
- Health
  - Alternative Health
  - Fitness & Nutrition
  - Self-Help
  - Sexuality

- Kids & Family
- Music
- News & Politics
- Religion & Spirituality
  - Buddhism
  - Christianity
  - Hinduism
  - Islam
  - Judaism
  - Other
  - Spirituality
- Science & Medicine
  - Medicine
  - Natural Sciences
  - Social Sciences
- Society & Culture
  - History
  - Personal Journals
  - Philosophy
  - Places & Travel
- Sports & Recreation
  - Amateur
  - College & High School
  - Outdoor
  - Professional
- Technology
  - Gadgets
  - Tech News
  - Podcasting
  - Software How-To
- TV & Film

- **Description.** Your show's description is very important. It is the *TV Guide*-style listing that people will read when they are browsing for new shows to try out. This is the one thing that influences prospective customers the most once they've landed on your podcast's page or entry in iTunes. They need to believe that your show is worth downloading and that it covers the subjects they're interested in. You are limited to 4000 characters (including spaces) for a description, but we recommend you keep it shorter than that. In our experience, a one- or two-paragraph description should be more than adequate. We strongly recommend you take a look at show descriptions for the top-rated shows in the category you intend to choose. Look for how different podcasters try to appeal to their customer base. Depending on the style of your show and its subject matter, your style of writing may vary.

The descriptive information about your podcast is the primary way a new subscriber finds and selects your podcast.

- **Keywords.** You can enter up to 12 keywords that help people searching for your podcast. These keywords are meant to supplement your show's description. iTunes will remove your podcast if it includes lists of irrelevant words in the itunes:summary, description, or itunes:keywords tags. Be sure you separate each keyword with a comma.

- **Episode Title.** The episode title is generally the name of the file you publish. We recommend using your show title as an acronym, followed by the episode number and a short title (e.g., PSV_76_Channels.m4v). This will indicate to new visitors that your show is serialized and makes it easier for them to spot unviewed content.
- **Episode Description.** The episode description generally appears below or next to a show's title. You can assign a description using up to 255 characters. Be sure to "get to the point" quickly and describe the content of the episode. This is also referred to as the subtitle.
- **Content Description.** This is a standard RSS 2.0 element that allows you to enter in show notes, messages, or other HTML-based content that you would like to have associated with your podcast. This is similar to the episode description element previously mentioned except that it is the section of your RSS feed that will be accessed by search engine robots and could help new listeners find your podcast. Show notes (essentially a transcription or outline of the show) should go in this section. This is very important because as of this date no reliable audio or video search engines exist.

Creating a Feed That's iTunes Friendly

Because the vast majority of users find podcasts using the iTunes client, it's a good idea to focus on achieving an iTunes-optimized feed. Apple offers the following advice about writing your feed.

- You need to pay very close attention to the title, author, description, and keywords tags at the <channel> level of your podcast feed. This is the information that is indexed for searches. This is also the copy that becomes your "packaging" in the store.
- Make your title specific. Apple says, "A podcast entitled 'Our Community Bulletin' is too vague and will attract no subscribers, no matter how compelling the content."
- The <itunes:summary> tag allows you to describe the show in great detail. Apple suggests telling your audience about the "subject matter, media format, episode schedule, and other relevant info so that they know what they'll be getting when they subscribe." A good idea is to create a list of search terms you think a user would enter, then building these into your podcast description.
- Minimize your use of keywords. iTunes favors the summary tag over keywords. iTunes recommends instead that you use keywords for things like misspellings of names or titles. To prevent the abuse of keywords, iTunes ignores all but the first 12 keywords you've entered.
- Make sure you assign a valid iTunes category (you can browse iTunes for a list of categories). This makes it more likely the show will appear in its appropriate category and makes it easier for casual browsers to find your program.

Developing Show Graphics

Your podcast needs a graphic to go with it. This artwork should be square-shaped and usable in a variety of ways. It will appear on the screen of the portable media player as well as in the podcast aggregator software. This is also the artwork used in the podcast directories. Having eye-catching artwork that helps brand your show is essential. This is often the first thing a person browsing sees ... so be sure you get it right.

Your show's graphic should help establish the show's subject matter and tone.

We recommend developing your artwork using a raster-based image editor like Adobe Photoshop and saved as a JPG or PNG. We recommend building the show's logo at 900 × 900 pixels so it is easier to see during the design stages. This has the added benefit that you can use the logo for print and promotional purposes. When you are ready to publish for iTunes, invoke Photoshop's Save for Web command. You can then resize to 400 × 400 pixels, which is Apple's preferred size. Check to see if the text is hard to read or the artwork looks too busy. Before you create your show artwork, browse the iTunes store and look at the artwork of the top-rated shows.

The "Really Small" Test

Apple recommends testing your show logo scaled down to 50 × 50 pixels. This is the size the graphic will display if you are added to the featured lists or many of the showcases.

Anatomy of a Feed

While we've identified many of the parts you'll need to write or make decisions on, let's take a look at a feed from a technical angle. The iTunes Store requires that a feed use RSS 2.0. You can also add some specialized tags that are highly useful in helping people find your podcast. These iTunes tags often repeat information already found in the feed, but they ensure compliance with iTunes specifications.

```
<?xml version="1.0" encoding="utf-8"?>
<rss xmlns:itunes="http://www.itunes.com/dtds/
podcast-1.0.dtd" version="2.0">
```

The RSS feed begins by identifying that it is using XML with UTF-8 encoding for your feed. Other encodings are not guaranteed to work in iTunes. The feed is also identified as using RSS version 2.0, which is needed for most podcasting aggregators.

Feed Tutorial with Sample Code

Looking for an in-depth tutorial on all the tags available in a feed as well as sample code to modify? Then be sure to check out How to Create RSS/XML Feed for Podcasts at www.podcast411.com/howto_1.html.

Channel Information

After the RSS feed is identified, you need to populate it with information about the channel. This information remains constant and should apply to all shows within the series.

```
<channel>
    <lastBuildDate>Mon, 12 Nov 2007 10:33:48 -0500
</lastBuildDate>
    <title>Secrets of Style with Kim Foley</title>
    <itunes:author>Kim Foley ‚Äì RHED Pixel
</itunes:author>
    <link>http://www.kimfoleystyle.com</link>
    <language>en</language>
    <copyright>©2008 RHED Pixel</copyright>
```

The feed then contains information about the channel; this includes a build date, which identifies when the feed was last modified, as well as the title and author of the show. You'll want to identify what language the show is published in (it is a global market after all) and specify who holds the show's copyright.

```
<itunes:summary>Want to be memorable, approachable
and exude confidence? If you are 40, 50, 60 or beyond
you will love this inspirational, detailed journey
showing you all the tricks and trade secrets of how
to look fabulous. Kim Foley, a television stylist for
over 25 years, shares all the secrets that make your
favorite Hollywood stars look great! She shares the
secrets of illusion dressing and spills the beans
on the techniques of television stylists. Watch the
```

```
podcast series for makeup techniques, hairstyle how
to&apos;s and clothing advice to really flatter your
figure.</itunes:summary>
```

This is the show's description. Remember, you are allowed up to 4000 characters to convince a potential viewer to watch.

```
<itunes:owner>
    <itunes:name>Kim Foley</itunes:name>
    <itunes:email>kfoley@nodmomain.net</itunes:email>
</itunes:owner>
```

This information is not visible in the directories, but is there so people can contact the podcast creator.

```
<itunes:image href="http://podcastingforacause.com/
kim.jpg" />
```

This is a URL for the show's logo. The image must be a JPEG or PNG file. Size the image to 400 × 400 pixels for maximum compatibility with iTunes.

```
<itunes:category text="Arts">
    <itunes:category text="Fashion &amp; Beauty"/>
    <itunes:keywords>Fashion, Beauty, Hair, Makeup,
Make-up, Fitness, Kim Foley,Kim Foly, Red Pixel,
RHED Pixel</itunes:keywords>
    <itunes:explicit>clean</itunes:explicit>
```

You should next identify the show's category or categories. Remember to use keywords to address misspellings or additional search criteria that aren't covered by the show's description. Lastly, you should categorize the show using one of three labels: <itunes:explict> yes, no, or clean. If you choose "yes," an "explicit" parental advisory graphic will appear next to your podcast artwork. If you choose "no" you will see no indicator. If you specify clean, then a "clean" graphic will appear.

Item Information

After the channel information comes the information for each episode (or item). This information provides a description of each episode. An accurate description is important because it motivates viewers to keep watching your shows.

```
<item>
    <title>Kim Foley - Makeup in Minutes</title>
    <itunes:author>Kim Foley ‚Äî RHED Pixel
</itunes:author>
            <itunes:subtitle>A two-minute makeup.
</itunes:subtitle>
            <itunes:summary> Television stylist
Kim Foley shows you a two-minute makeup that will
give you a polished look when you&apos;re running
out of time.</itunes:summary>
```

This information contains the description for each episode. Be detailed, but remember you have a 255-character limit for each item.

```
<enclosure type="video/mp4" url=" http://media.
podhoster.com/photoshop/Kim_Episode_4.mp4"
length="17977053" />
```

The <enclosure> tag must have three attributes:

- **Type.** What kind of file the enclosure is. iTunes supports the extensions m4a, mp3, mov, mp4, m4v, and pdf. Other aggregators may support additional file types.
- **URL.** Identifies where the file lives on a server.
- **Length.** The length attribute is the file size in bytes.

```
<guid>http://media.podhoster.com/photoshop/
Kim_Episode_4.mp4</guid>
     <pubDate>Mon, 12 Nov 2007 10:26:05 -0500</pubDate>
     <itunes:explicit>clean</itunes:explicit>
     <itunes:duration>00:01:31</itunes:duration>
     <itunes:keywords>Fashion, Beauty, Hair, Makeup,
Kim Foley </itunes:keywords>
```

Every item in your feed must have a unique identifier that never changes. This *g*lobal *u*ser *id*entification (or guid) is used to determine which episodes are new. Most people choose to use the episode URL for the guid value. You can also add information about the file, including its publication date, duration, and additional keywords.

```
     </item>
```

At the end of an item you must close the item off with the end tag </item>. You can then start over and insert additional items to the feed.

Programming the Feed

There are several ways to create a podcast feed. Which method you choose will depend on your skill level with RSS and your personal preference. Some people enjoy hand-coding their feed, while others want to do everything with a web browser. There is no right way—it depends on each situation—but here's an overview of your options and some suggestions about when to use each method.

Hand-Coding RSS

Many podcasters choose to hand-code their RSS feed. If you have a background in web design or programming, then this is a perfectly valid approach. You'll find a sample feed on the iTunes tech spec page: www.apple.com/itunes/store/podcaststechspecs. html#example.

Unsupported Formats

If the file extension of the URL attribute is not supported, your episode will not appear in a podcast directory.

The benefits of this approach are that it will deepen your understanding of what is really happening with your files and that it will give you precise control. The drawbacks are that it you may have to learn a new programming language and that it can be time-consuming.

We may sound wimpy, but we're not big fans of hand-coding. We recommend using a tool to generate your RSS feed. Then learn to read and analyze your feed as errors arise.

Blog-based Solutions

Using a blog software tool is a very easy way to publish a podcast. Blog software is both affordable and easy to use. Remember that a podcast is essentially a blog with audio or video. This is probably the easiest way to create your RSS feed (especially if you want a website to go along with your show).

In order to generate the feed you can add an entry (or post) to your blog. The post on your blog can contain show notes (essentially an outline of the show) as well as any weblinks or resources. This has the added benefit that many users choose to subscribe to blogs with email notification. In this way you can notify viewers who prefer to browse podcasts via a web browser. The steps for

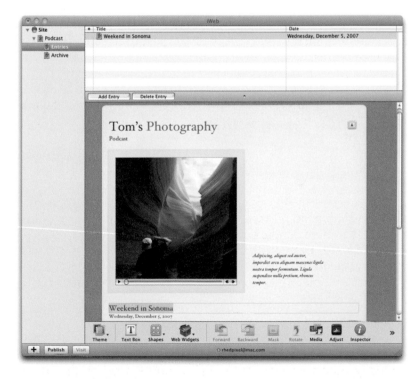

iWeb is a useful application for creating blogs and podcast feeds. It is an easy-to-use application that is good for newer users and those looking for a simple solution.

Blog Often If You Want Success

There's a strong correlation between the aging and post frequency of blogs and their authority ranking. "A-list" bloggers tend to post at least twice a day and therefore have more "authority" on Technorati (a blog search engine).

creating a podcast from a blog feed vary slightly depending on the software tool used but are very well documented in the support forums or online documentation for each tool.

There are dozens of tools for creating blogs. Some are free, such as the web-based Blogger. Others are full-featured and require you to install components on your web server. A good comparison of popular blogging tools can be found at www.ojr.org/ojr/images/blog_software_comparison.cfm.

If you are looking for the easiest technical approach, try a hosted blog solution. These can be active within minutes and don't require you to set up hosting for the blog (you still need hosting for your podcast media). The solutions can have monthly charges, so be sure to explore your options fully. The three most popular hosted blogs are

- **TypePad** (www.typepad.com)
- **Blogger** (www.blogger.com)
- **LiveJournal** (www.livejournal.com)

If you host your own blog, you can gain greater control. There are several tools that can work with new or existing web hosts. Some of the most popular software tools include

- **Movable Type** (www.movabletype.org)
- **WordPress** (www.wordpress.org)
- **RapidWeaver** (www.realmacsoftware.com)
- **iWeb** (www.apple.com/ilife/iweb)
- **Contribute** (www.adobe.com/products/contribute)

A Short History of Blogging

In order to better understand podcasting you need to understand blogging. Essentially podcasting is an extension of blogging (which is why some folks still refer to podcasts as audio and video blogging).

It was 1994 when we actually saw Mosaic Web Browsers, the ability for the web to have pictures. The year 1994 is also recognized as the start of blogging. A college student named Justin Hall had a website called www.links.net. Justin Hall decided to put up what he called Lessons from Life on a pretty much daily basis, and he would just do a daily entry about things that he discovered that day or things that he found online. And the concept of doing routine content that could be sifted and sorted by date and topic began to evolve.

- In 1996, Dave Winer did a blog for the 24 Hour Democracy Project and this is seen as one of the most successful instances of somebody really formalizing a blog and pulling in multiple sources.
- In 1999, the first blogging software, called Blogger, came out that tried to make blogging mass market.
- In 2002, Gizmodo emerged and was seen as the first blog empire. Gizmodo started collecting blogs and had bloggers working together. It was the equivalent of a network and facilitated the selling of ads for the pages.
- In 2003, political blogs took off. Many politicians use their blogs to speak directly to their constituents and supporters.

The history of blogging is certainly deeper than this short overview. We highly encourage you to dig deeper and explore the culture and history of blogging.

Web-based Solutions

Many podcasters choose to use web-based solutions to generate their RSS feeds. Most podcast-hosting companies include browser-based tools that make it easy to upload your files and generate your RSS feed at the same time. We evaluated several podcast hosting companies in our last chapter, and all but one provided ways to create feeds using a web browser.

The major benefits of these web-based tools are ease of use and compatibility. Because the tools are designed for non-programmers, they prompt you to enter all of the required information. This approach practically guarantees a compatible feed; it can also open up many other options. Several hosting companies optimize the feeds and make it easier by adding one-click subscriptions and email subscription lists.

The principle drawback of using browser-based approaches is a lack of speed. Entering information manually can create a lot of repetition. If you have to load several episodes at once, the browser option generally limits you to a single upload at a time (which can result in a lot of waiting time).

If you're new to podcasting, and are not prepared to invest the extra time in a blog, then browser-based solutions are generally the best fit.

One-Click Zune Podcast Link Builder

Want a one-click button that lets your readers subscribe to your podcast in the Zune Marketplace? Then visit www.zunepodcastsubscription.com/.

WYSIWYG Solutions

As podcasting's popularity has grown, a new crop of software tools has emerged. WYSIWYG is an acronym that stands for "what you see is what you get," and that's exactly what these tools do. Several software developers have released RSS podcasting tools. The two most notable are Podcast Maker for the Mac (www. lemonzdream.com/podcastmaker) and The Podcast RSS Buddy for PC and Mac (www.tolley.info/rssbuddy).

Both of these tools offer an easy-to-use interface. They also let you simulate how the podcast will look in iTunes. Both programs generate a standard feed as well as an optimized version with the iTunes tags. Both tools are easy to use. Podcast Maker offers the extra benefit of having an FTP program built in, which speeds up the publishing process.

These solutions are best for podcasters who need to publish several episodes in a short time period. These give you the ability to control the feed creation process with the safety net of a preview feature. The drawback is that both of these tools have very small development teams, so if you encounter problems or errors, you can't expect the level of support that a major developer would offer. With that said, we have found both of these products to be reliable and easy to use.

Need to Move a Feed?

It is not uncommon to need to move a feed from time to time as your podcast evolves. This could be due to server upgrades or a change in your podcast's website. This is why the <itunes:new-feed-url> tag exists.

This tag allows you to change the URL where the podcast feed is located without having to cancel and resubmit your feed. You can add this item at <channel> level and it lets you redirect both iTunes and subscribers.

```
<itunes:new-feed-url>http://podcastingforacause.com/example.rss</itunes:
new-feed-url>
```

After adding the tag to your old feed, leave it in place for at least 48 hours (the recommended time is 2 weeks). You can then retire the old feed because iTunes will have updated its listings. For more information see www.apple.com/itunes/store/podcast-stechspecs.html#changing

For other redirects you'll use a HTTP 301 response. For details, see www.somacon.com/p145.php.

Publishing the Feed

Once your feed is built, it needs to be published and submitted to the appropriate directories. The process is straightforward, but must be executed with care and precision. If you make mistakes, your show can be delayed or blocked.

Testing the Feed

There are lots of things that can break a feed. A misplaced character, a malformed date, the list goes on. Fortunately, testing a feed is easy. Once you have your feed and media available online, you'll want to test it. The easiest way is to visit www.feedvalidator.org, where you can enter the address for your feed. If there are errors in your feed, they will be clearly identified. The website also offers suggestions and links to more information on how to fix common problems. This website is invaluable and should be a part of your testing process.

Once you think a feed is working, you should test it with the iTunes client. Before you submit the feed to directories for listing, follow this easy process:

1. Launch the iTunes application.
2. In the Advanced menu, choose Subscribe to Podcast.

Feed Validator helps identify errors with your RSS feed and suggests repairs you can make to improve compatibility.

The Difference Between the iTunes Client and the iTunes Store

You'll often see the word *iTunes* used to mean several things. The first meaning is a software application that allows Mac and PC users to manage music, movies, podcasts, and TV shows. The program can help organize a large media library and allows you to transfer content to devices like iPods, iPhones, and Apple TV.

The other meaning is an online site called the iTunes Store. This allows users to browse for purchase content as well as free podcasts. When you submit a podcast to the iTunes Store you are asking it to display your RSS feed in the appropriate category and to make it searchable. If your feed is accepted, the iTunes Store updates the podcast directory with new or updated information about your podcast.

Once user subscribe to your podcast, they no longer need to access it through the iTunes Store. Instead, it will be added to the Podcasts tab in their Library. The feed is checked directly from your sever and the media is downloaded from your server.

Email Subscriptions

While it may seem counterintuitive, many viewers want to be notified via email when a new podcast episode comes out. Be sure to take advantage of the email list options offered by FeedBurner and several podcast hosting companies.

3. Enter your feed URL in the text box.
4. Click the OK button.

If things are set up correctly, the podcast will be added to your Podcast playlist, which shows all the episodes you are subscribed to. If you see an orange circle next to the new podcast description, it means that iTunes is successfully downloading the most recent episode. When the orange circle disappears, the episode has been downloaded. Double-click to play the selected episode. If the episode successfully plays, your RSS feed and media are iTunes-compliant and should be submitted to podcasting directories.

Optimizing the Feed

Once your feed is valid, you can optimize it for greater compatibility and exposure. A popular service is FeedBurner (www.feedburner.com), which is now owned by Google. FeedBurner offers several free services, and since Google's purchase, the pro features are now free as well.

FeedBurner optimizes a standard RSS feed and adds several important features. FeedBurner publicizes your feed and offers tools that make it easier for people to subscribe. The feed is also optimized so it is ready for other web services such as digg, Yahoo, del.icio.us, Google, and AOL. Most importantly, it provides detailed traffic information so you can analyze your feed and who is consuming it.

If you are creating your feed by hand or with a blogging or WYSIWYG tool, FeedBurner can make the feed podcast-ready. The feed is also optimized for web browsers, can be subscribed to via email, and has multiple social media options enabled.

PRO*file*: The Rest of Everest

The Rest of Everest is a video podcast conceived and created by documentary filmmaker Jon Miller of TreeLine Productions (www.treelineproductions.com). It is "the rest" of the footage from the groundbreaking expedition documentary "Everest: The Other Side," which engrossed thousands of viewers when it premiered on Dish Network Pay-Per-View in May 2005.

The film documents the 2003 expedition to the Northeast Ridge route in Tibet and coincides with the 50th-anniversary climbing season. The story revolves around 23-year old climber Ben Clark and the fulfillment of his dream to become one of the youngest climbers ever to summit Everest. Although the film has been very well received, much of the story remained yet to be told.

"I had recently finished the edit on my own film about climbing Everest and thought it was such a shame that I had all of this material on tape that would never see the light of day," says Miller. "Surely there was a group of people who were interested in seeing hours and hours of Everest that no one ever shows?"

Miller returned from Everest with over 80 hours of tape from the 60-day expedition. The final cut of the film totaled just 84 minutes. That meant that only one minute of every hour filmed made it into the finished version. Miller was looking for a way to get his footage out there.

"In [the] fall of 2005 I watched my first video podcast, Four Eyed Monsters. It was a show about the trials and tribulations about promoting an independently produced film," Miller remembers. "The podcast really flipped a switch in my head. I thought the podcast was as engrossing as the film it was based on could ever be. I realized that podcasting was an entire ecosystem. A podcast could exist on its own for its own sake."

The Rest of Everest features nearly all of the footage from the trip. Additionally, Clark, the climber, and others offer audio commentary. This lets the viewer get all of the stories right from the people who experienced the climb firsthand. This new approach really connected with the audience.

"Podcasting has doubled my workload … and in a mostly unpaid way. But I love it and wouldn't change a thing," says Miller. "The show had introduced me to so many amazing people who simply found the show in iTunes through Google. Every morning I get up and check my email first thing to see who has written me while I was asleep. Podcasting is international in nature so I regularly get emails from Australia and Japan, Europe, and all over the USA. I make it a point to write back to every single person."

"It was these emails and friendships that I developed that made me realize that I was going to produce the show even if my viewership dropped down to just these people. It was for them. After I made that perspective change, the show has been a much more enjoyable endeavor. I still check stats, but I'm surprised to find that it can be up to a month between logins."

Miller encourages other media professionals to give podcasting a try. He emphasizes how enjoyable the entire process is.

Miller's passion for his show and its audience has been key to its success. Besides staying in the top-rated list for his podcast, he's received several honors for his show. "The Rest of Everest" was a finalist for the Best Video Podcast at the 2007 People's Choice Podcast Awards. The show was also designated by the iTunes directory as one of their exclusive Best of 2006podcasts.

"I was absolutely stats-obsessed when I began the show. I stayed that way for most of the first year. I'd check my download stats hourly through most of the day. At some point that all changed and I began to slow down on my obsessive-compulsive behavior. I knew I was producing a quality show and people, viewers, had noticed it as well," Miller explains. "I began to build relationships with several of the bigger fans. People started emailing me to say how the show had inspired them to travel or to climb the mountain outside of their town."

Recording Commentary Tracks

Many podcasters will need to record their guests' audio via telephone. Miller shared his process for recording commentary tracks for video podcasts.

"First, I use Skype for recording the commentary to my episodes with guests," says Miller. "Since most of my guests are computer illiterate I can still use Skype-Out to call them on their landlines and get clean audio. The show would not be possible without Skype."

"To record the Skype calls on my Macs I use a little $15 application called Call Recorder. It plugs into Skype and allows me to record both sides of the conversation as uncompressed audio to separate tracks. That way I can edit the audio in post and everyone stays separate until I export the episode and do a mixdown. Call Recorder just works."

"I've been a professional content producer for over 10 years now and I can say that podcasting is the most gratifying endeavor I've ever undertaken," he says. "There's just something magical about being able to shoot, edit, and publish all by yourself and in such an immediate, international way. It's changed my life for the better. I'm happy to be a part of the podcasting community."

Gear List

- Sony HVR-A1U and HVR-V1U cameras ("I'm a real fan of tape since my productions take me to remote areas.")
- Libec TH-M20 tripod
- AKG C414 microphone
- Mackie 1402-VLZ PRO mixer
- Ultrasone HFI-550 headphones

PUBLISHING AND PROMOTING THE FEED

Once you've successfully built your podcast feed you'll need to register it with several podcast search engines. This is how new audience members can find you and subscribe to the show. But simply putting your podcast in a directory will not draw in large crowds. You'll need to take steps to promote your podcast and do so in a way that effectively attracts people who'll be interested in your content.

A valid RSS feed is required for your podcast.

Submitting the Feed

Before you submit your feed to directories, it needs to be working properly. If your feed is not working and validated, as we discussed in the last chapter, your show could be blocked from directory sites.

Submitting the Feed to iTunes

When a podcast is ready, you need to submit it for inclusion. The first place you submit should be the iTunes Store (this is where your biggest audience will come from). If, when you are testing the feed, you can subscribe to your podcast using the Advanced menu, then your show is ready to submit. In order to register a podcast on iTunes, you'll need to have a valid iTunes account (which requires a valid credit card, but you won't be charged unless you make purchases). Apple requires users to log in, which increases the likelihood the user's contact information will be valid.

1. Launch the iTunes application.
2. Click the iTunes Store icon in your sources list in the left column.
3. In the left navigation column, in the iTunes Store box, click the Podcasts link to go to the Podcasts page.
4. Scroll to the bottom of the page. In the Learn More box in the bottom left corner, click the Submit a Podcast link.
5. Follow the instructions on the Submit a Podcast page. You will need to have your podcast feed URL ready.

6. If you are not logged in, iTunes will prompt you to do so before accepting your submission.
7. If your RSS feed is valid and has all of the recommended iTunes tags, you will see a summary page after you submit your feed URL. If some of the required items are missing, iTunes will prompt you to fill them in.

Submit to More Directories

While the iTunes Store has about 70% of the market for podcast subscriptions, it's not the only game in town. There are several more podcast directories on the market. Some are for special interests like religion or family-friendly content. You can find a useful directory at www.masternewmedia.org/podcast_directory.

The podcast directories we recommend submitting to are as follows:

- **Podcast Alley** (www.podcastalley.com)
- **Zune Marketplace** (www.zune.net)
- **Podcast Directory** (www.podcastdirectory.com)
- **Podcast Alley** (www.podcastalley.com)
- **Podcast.net** (www.podcast.net)
- **Odeo.com** (www.Odeo.com)
- **iPodder.org** (www.iPodder.org)
- **Podcast Pickle** (www.podcastpickle.com)
- **MeFeedia** (www.mefeedia.com)

Advice on Succeeding in the iTunes Store from Apple

Looking for some helpful tips on how to succeed in the iTunes Store? Apple offers a useful video called *The Podcast Recipe: Producing a Successful Show*. They promote this as an opportunity "find out what it takes to perform a great-sounding podcast, produce a professional show, and promote a podcast to reach as many people as possible."

The online seminar is free. (www.seminars.apple.com/seminarsonline/podcast/apple/index.html)

You Must Submit

With over 100,000 podcasts in existence, and that number growing fast, one of the best ways for people to find content that interests them is in the podcast directories. There are dozens of directories for podcasts. Be sure to register in as many as you can, starting with iTunes and Zune Marketplace.

The Submission Queue

Once you submit a podcast to the iTunes Store, it needs to be reviewed. Depending on the number of shows submitted, this could take awhile. iTunes actually has its shows reviewed by live humans. The same holds true for other directories like Zune Marketplace.

If you want to ensure your podcast makes it out of the approval queue, check the following issues:

- Are there any technical problems with the feed? This includes a lack of episodes or the inability to download or play episodes from the host server.
- Do you require a login or password? If you require a login or password to access your feed, it will be blocked from the iTunes Store.
- Does your podcast include a large amount of sexual content or a title that uses explicit language? If so, your show will be rejected. You *can* use explicit language in a show, but it must be labeled as explicit.
- Have you misused copyrighted material? If you misrepresent Apple copyrights, including "iPod" or "iTunes," your show will be blocked. This includes using an image of an iPod in your show artwork.
- Could your content be considered offensive? Material that is deemed offensive, such as racist content or child pornography, is not allowed in the iTunes Store.

Addressing the above issues is a good idea before you submit to any other podcast directory as well. Keep in mind that all listings will take some time to appear. For example, it can take an average of five days for a listing to appear in the browseable categories of the iTunes Store. Your show's logo can take even longer to appear because images must be cached, then propagated across multiple servers.

How to Jump the Queue

If you are on a deadline and need your feed to be live by a certain date … start early. When pressed for time, we build our feed very early. Even if the first episodes aren't ready, we cut together a promotional trailer that explains the concept of the show and offers a taste of what's to come. Most directories will block "test" feeds … so make yours real and populate it with a trailer. Your feed will be ready to go when you need it.

Promotion Strategies

Successfully promoting a podcast is a challenging activity. There are many ways to approach the issue of raising awareness. The ideas contained in this chapter are drawn from our personal experiences as well as those of two respected experts. Special thanks to Jason Van Orden, prolific podcaster and author of *Promoting Your Pod-cast*, and Paul Vogelzang, who is part of the *MommyCast & Friends Channel* (www.mommycastandfriends. com), a very successful podcast network that creates content for families.

© istockphoto

Start with an Informative and Compelling Title for Your Podcast

Your title is most likely the first exposure someone will have to your podcast. There truly is something to the saying "You only have one chance to make a good first impression." Your podcast's title has only a few seconds to attract your target audience, grab their attention, and make them want to watch or listen. A good title instantly tells people what your show is about. Avoid "clever" puns that people have to think about.

Align Your Podcast with Key Media Partners

New media cannot ignore traditional media. Similarly, traditional media is struggling to adapt to and adopt new media techniques. How can the two help each other? The simple answer is to build a bridge. By aligning your show with traditional media outlets, you can increase your reach. Podcasters can write magazine columns, serve as forum moderators for online message boards, or interview subjects for local news. It's important to realize that most people still turn to traditional media; you can't ignore its reach. Podcasters who partner can get a lot further than those who attempt to do everything on their own.

Cross-Promote with Other Internet Shows

An effective way to find potential listeners is to target the audiences of shows that are similar to your own. Most podcasters don't believe in the pie theory, which says there's an infinite number of listeners that can only be divided so many ways.

A Great Book on Podcast Promotion

Promoting your podcast is essential to its long-term success. While we've explored several ideas in this chapter, we highly recommend *Promoting Your Podcast* by Jason Van Orden. You can find out more on the book at www.promotingyourpodcast.com.

iTunes Searching: How Will You Be Discovered?

There are three ways a potential subscriber can find you in the iTunes Store. Understanding the three methods is important if you want to improve your chances of being found.

1. **Search.** The iTunes Store contains a search field. Results are returned based on popularity and relevance. Popularity relates to the number of new subscribers you've had in a given period (which is an uncontrollable factor). Relevance is due largely to your show's description and keywords (which you have complete control over). Be sure to write an accurate description that addresses your show's topic. You can also use keywords to address misspellings or additional search criteria.

2. **Featured Content.** The iTunes Store routinely features content. There are several factors that contribute to a show being featured. First and foremost, the quality of content is considered. Second, your show must have attractive artwork (which does not include Apple items like logos or iPods). The staff at the iTunes Store also favor shows with consistent content that is released regularly (e.g., weekly or daily). It should also go without saying that your feed needs to be valid, so periodically check it at www.feedvalidator.org.

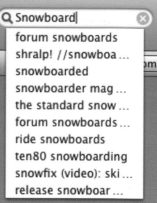

3. **Top Lists.** On each page of the iTunes Store there is a "Top List." These lists showcase the top shows in each category. Making these lists is based on new subscriptions. We often recommend launching a show with four episodes (simply pre-date the first three to offset their "release"). This way a new show offers visitors multiple options. This initial surge can help you make a splash. Once you are on a Top List, it is essential you maintain your release schedule and quality. Staying on a Top List is very helpful, as it makes it much easier for visitors to discover your show.

Therefore, many podcasters are willing to share their audiences through cross-promotion strategies.

Podcasters enjoy using content from outside sources to make their shows more interesting. Find shows that relate to your topic, then contribute content that adds value to those shows and that promotes your show at the same time, here are some suggestions:

- Offer to be a guest on other podcasters's shows, and then return the favor by inviting them on your show.
- Produce guest segments or serve as a field producer for another podcast.
- Add questions or comment to other show's blogs. Be sure your show is mentioned in your signature line.
- Consider exchanging show promotional announcements with other podcasters.

Search-Engine-Optimize Your Podcast's Site

There are many things you can do to make your podcast more search-engine friendly. The goal is to make your site appear as relevant and authoritative as possible. The good news is that search engines like sites that are frequently updated (which your podcast blog should be).

Unfortunately, the major search engines do not watch and index your video content. This makes the text content extremely

> **Publish Your Podcast with a Blog**
>
> We emphasized this a lot in our last chapter, but it bears repeating. You should use a blog platform to publish your podcast. It is the easiest way to create an RSS feed. It also provides a great "home base" for your podcast where listeners can find archived shows and comment on each episode. Blogs are very search-engine friendly.

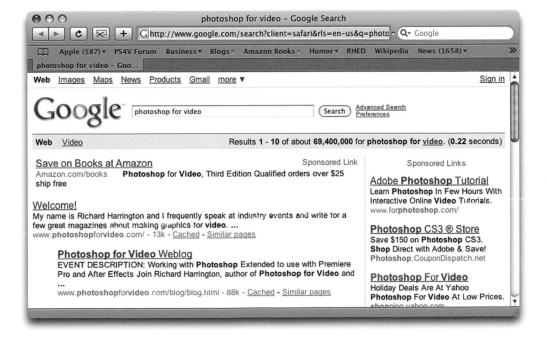

Want to Put Your Podcast on Video Sharing Sites?

Many podcasters choose to put selected episodes on video sharing sites like YouTube. While it's generally a bad idea to put all your podcasts up on these sites (it will drive down your subscription numbers), they are good for promotional impact.

important. Be sure to include textual show notes for each episode—detailed descriptions and content outlines that let readers and the search engines know what each episode is about. For even better ranking, consider posting transcripts of your show to provide additional text content that search engines can index.

Automatically Notify Directories about New Content

Each time you post a new episode of your show, you want several directories to immediately crawl, index, and list the new content. The easiest way to make sure this happens is to send an instant notification, called a "ping." If you use a blog to publish your show, the blog software can be configured to do this for you automatically, each time you post a new episode. Another option is to visit www.pingomatic.com each time you post new content. Submit your feed and Pingomatic will automatically notify the most important directories. If you don't manually ping the directories, it can take a few days for new content to appear.

Increase Inbound Links to Your Site

The more other websites link to your content, the more authority you have on the Internet. More authority leads to a higher search ranking, which in turn leads to more traffic and more inbound links. The simple truth is that most people don't make it beyond the first few hits on a web search.

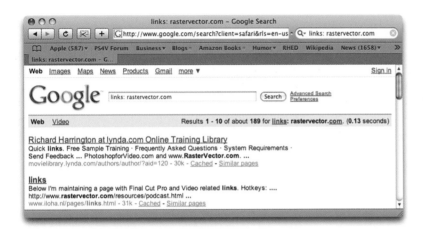

You can do a web search using "links: your_url.com" (substituting your own URL) to see who's linking to your site.

The best way to encourage links to your site is to regularly publish quality content. Find directories that allow you to submit your web address. Develop relationships with bloggers and podcasters who publish related content and might want to link back to you. Include links to your site when you participate in blog commenting and forum posting. You'll want to build several paths to your website (just be sure you return the favor to those who help you).

Make It Easy for People to Share and Bookmark Your Content

The viral nature of social networks has created a marketing nirvana. People can instantly share content with their entire social circle. By making it easy for your audience to share your content on popular social networks you will increase the reach of

If you enjoyed this article, please bookmark/share it:

Digg   del.icio.us   Reddit   StumbleUpon

You can add social network buttons to your blog to make it easier for people to share and comment on your podcasts and posts.

Want to Post to Several Video-Sharing Sites at Once?

If you are looking for an easy way to post your video to several sites, then take a look at TubeMogul (www.tubemogul.com). With a single upload, your video can be added to YouTube, Google Video, Revver, and more. Plus you get tracking statistics that can help you understand your viewership.

Metadata Is Essential

You show needs good metadata so people can find your podcast. This includes all of the information that describes your podcast to the potential subscriber, as well as to podcast directories.

Besides your show's title, author, and description, you can use up to 12 keywords to determine relevance. A high percentage of potential subscribers look for podcasts using searchable directories. If you don't have useful, robust metadata, your podcast will not turn up.

your show. Popular social networks include Digg.com, Del.icio. us, Facebook.com, and StumbleUpon.com. These sites provide bookmark widgets that you can include on your site so visitors can share your content with one click. These are a very good idea to add to your show's blog.

Advertise and Promote

This may sound obvious, but you need to promote your show. This includes running ads in traditional venues like magazines or websites. One technique we employ is creating a business card for each of our podcast series. In this way, when we talk up the show with people we meet, they can easily remember the show name and blog when they get to their computer. You don't need to spend a fortune on advertising—many podcasters trade ads with one another, placing ads in their shows for certain products or events, then asking for links or ads in exchange.

Aggregate Your Content

If you produce multiple podcasts that could appeal to the same audience, then be sure you aggregate and cross-promote. For example, you can list other shows on your podcast's blog page. We often add blog posts about other shows to promote crossover content that should appeal.

You can also create an artist page on iTunes. This is a single page that lists all your shows in one place. Simply click on the Report a Concern button, and select Remove a Podcast. In the dialog box, explain that you would like an artist page, give them the exact name of the artist (don't include "Inc," "LLC," etc.), and list the exact feed URLs or links to your podcasts. Note that a podcast can only appear on one artist page.

You can request a single page to show all of your podcasts in one place.

Building a Relationship with Your Audience

While attracting new subscribers is important, long-term success comes from maintaining the subscribers you already have. To do this, you must build a meaningful relationship with your audience. Here are a few ways to connect and build on that connection.

Stay Focused

What is your show all about? Perhaps you should write it down "for the record." Many podcasters struggle to come up with new show topics. As such, their shows drift away from the intended topic (and subsequently lose both their focus and their viewers). One recommended technique is mind-mapping, which involves visually organizing information. You can essentially start with a few core topics and keep breaking them down into related ideas to come up with new show topics. You can find out more on mind-mapping at www.en.wikipedia.org/wiki/Mind_map.

©istockphoto

A mind map can help you identify possible show topics.

Remember Who Listens

Do you know who watches your podcast? Be sure you have a target audience in mind when you develop show ideas. One thing we find useful is to look at our podcast page in iTunes. Here we can see a section called "Listeners Also Subscribed To." You can follow the links listed there and discover what other shows are being consumed by your listeners. This can help you develop an overview of what your audience is interested in.

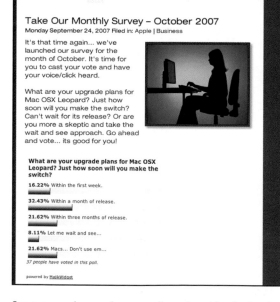

Surveys are a fun way for your audience to get involved and a useful way for you to better understand your viewers.

Interact with Your Audience

You want to provide your audience a way to speak back to you. This can mean an email address or voice mail line. Another way is to allow commenting on your blog or allow forums. When your audience members speak up, answer them. Include their comments in the show. Thank them for participating. Respond to what they say.

You should also include surveys on your website or blog. We frequently use the survey tools from MajikWidget (www.majikwidget. com). Others employ the more detailed Survey Monkey (www.surveymonkey.com). Whatever technology you use, people like having a chance to voice their opinion.

Listen to Other Shows in Your Space

Do you know what your show's competition is? It's important to periodically check out what other shows are doing. You can learn a lot by analyzing shows that are ranked both above and below yours. You'll want to look at them for ideas on content and approach.

In some ways you can counter-program. For example, if your competition is fairly dry, you can integrate light humor. If other shows are very long, try taking the abbreviated approach. What you should do is analyze the market, looking for both ways to make your show stand out and best practices.

Build Your Brand and Host Recognition

We have found that establishing credibility and building a brand have been very helpful in the long run. Podcast hosts should look to improve their "terrestrial" credibility by speaking at conferences as well as offering interviews to traditional media.

We also find that showing the host on camera works well. Be sure to give some face time to your host, rather than just focusing on the subject of an interview or source of a technical demonstration.

Make It Easy to Subscribe

It is important that you make subscriptions easy. This means you need to recognize that your audience may have different desires regarding technology than you. Make sure that you offer both RSS subscriptions and one-click subscribe buttons for several popular formats. Usually your host company can help with this; if not, you should harness the power of FeedBurner (www.feedburner.com). You'll also want to give people the option to subscribe via an email list. A surprising number of folks still want to be emailed when new episodes come out.

Potential Revenue from Your Podcast

Because we're sure it's all on your mind ... let's talk briefly about monetizing your podcast. Perhaps your goal is to make enough for the podcast to fund itself ... maybe you'd like to go further and see this as an extra source of income. Either way, you won't get there overnight.

What we offer here are a few starting points. These are some proven ways you can monetize your podcast content.

Advertising

If you have a large viewership, then you can explore ad sponsorship services. There are several in this space, such as Podango, Podtrac, and Kliptronic. The rates earned will vary based on your show's subject matter and audience size. Most of these services will sell ads for you, and then keep a percentage of the sales.

You can go and sell your own ads, which is more work but you keep more money. If you want to seek a sponsor, you'll need to put together a media kit that showcases the strength of your podcast and accurately describes its audience (both in size and in demographics).

None of the podcast directories have an issue with shows that contain ads. We recommend keeping ads short and to the point.

Amazon Associate

Many people will produce a podcast that mentions particular products (such as technology, books, film, or music). There is one online retailer who does a great job selling all of these, Amazon. com. If your show has a blog or website, you can provide a list of the featured products. For example, if your podcast talks about a piece of software or a book, and you link to Amazon to buy it, you can get paid. Simply sign up for an Amazon Associates account (www.affiliate-program.amazon.com). Amazon pays you up to 10% commission on everything you sell as a click-through on

---

More on Making Money from Podcasting

 There are a few sources we respect for ideas on making money from podcasts.

- **Podcasting for Profit** (www.leesabarnesbooktour.com)
- **The Podcasting** Underground (www.podcastingunderground.com)
- **Online Media Success Podcast** (www.onlinemediasuccess.com)
- **Internet Business** Mastery (www.internetbusinessmastery.com)
- **The Business of Podcasting and New Media** (www.paulcolligan.com)
- *Podcast Academy: The Business Podcasting Book: Launching, Marketing, and Measuring Your Podcast* by Michael Geoghegan, Greg Cangialosi, Ryan Irelan, and Tim Bourquin

your website. Additionally, if someone who clicks through does any other shopping there, you get a percentage of that purchase as well. This is an easy way to bring in revenue that can offset or even cover costs associated with a podcast.

iTunes Affiliate

In a move similar to the Amazon Associate model, Apple offers the iTunes Affiliate program. If you create a link to it in your own, it can take visitors to the iTunes Store. You can then earn a 5% commission on sales of songs, movies, TV shows, and audiobooks purchased by customers who linked to the iTunes Store from your website. Anything they purchase during the next 24 hours will be credited to your affiliate account. The iTunes Affiliate program is only available in selected countries (www.apple.com/itunes/affiliates/).

Website Ads and Google AdSense

Many podcasters choose to place ads on their websites. For some, this takes the form of banner ads from show sponsors. Others take the easier approach of allowing Google AdSense ads into their blogs. These are generally text-only links and can be placed in the sidebar area of a website. An easy way to add these to your blog is by using FeedBurner (www.feedburner.com).

Selling Back Episodes

Many podcasters look to make money from their catalog of materials. Some do this by bundling back episodes together and selling them on DVD at full quality. Others make back episodes available for sale or through subscription only. Another option is to produce short podcasts, and then offer more in-depth materials for sale. Many see podcasts as a brand builder, something that can be used to pull in new people and sell related products or services.

The Road Ahead

The world of podcasting will continue to evolve at a rapid pace. In order to keep this book relevant, please visit our companion website, www.VidPodcaster.com. Here you'll find a blog, as well as a podcast and several video tutorials. This is where we'll keep the book up-to-date as technology evolves.

To access exclusive content, you'll need the following information.
username: video
password: podcaster

INDEX